Thank God!! :)
We're debt free!!
$83,900 in
20 months
-Jesse + Jenn

Michelle
35K in
...001
...ere
Thank you so much debt free!!
Dave! You are really
an inspiration to
so many!

Erin & Kevin
Phoenix, AZ

Kyle + Amber White
$36,000 in 7 months!
Say NO to debt!!

$51,000 PAID OFF
AT 51 YEARS OLD!
I am debt free!
Elaine Davidson

WE'RE DEBT FREE!
THANKS FOR EVERYTHING
DAVE!
Mike & Cathy

To God Be The Glory!
We're Debt FREE!!!
The Schmersal Family!
$120,000.00 Paid off 34mths!
William
Luke
M
Faith
Rebekah
Lydia
Rob ♡ Anji

Debt free!
-Jen & Jim

Dave and Kim Monk (Troy, IL)
$137,000 in 3½ years!
* including our home! :)
☑ Baby step 6

We're debt free!
119,500/35 mo
We did it, So can you
Stephanie & David

THIS BOOK BELONGS TO

YOU ARE ABOUT TO Change LIVES

As a coordinator, you're not just leading a money course.

You're helping change lives! You're joining us on our mission to bring hope to people in every walk of life, no matter where they are on their financial journey.

You'll meet a single mom just trying to get by. You'll get to know a businessman who drives a car he can't afford to a job he doesn't like to earn a paycheck he sends to someone else. You'll connect with a young couple drowning in student loans and an older couple worried that they won't be able to retire with dignity.

You're about to intersect their lives and share hope like they've never felt before. Thank you!

You may be feeling a little nervous, but don't worry. You don't have to be a financial expert. In fact, Chris, Rachel, and I will be handling all the teaching. Your job is to encourage, love, and support the members of your class. You'll walk them through discussions and activities, hear their stories, feel their hurts, challenge their bad habits, and inspire them to change their lives!

More than five million people over two decades have proved that anyone can win with money! Get ready because everyone in your class will come away changed forever—and that includes you.

I'm so proud of you. Thank you again for helping us change lives, and welcome to the *Financial Peace University* team!

It's game on!

LET'S DO THIS!

SOMEONE'S LIFE WILL CHANGE BECAUSE OF YOU. IT STARTS HERE.

TABLE OF *Contents*

THE 7 BABY STEPS

OUR *Proven* PLAN

If you want to win with money, you can't do what you've always done. You need a plan that works. That's why Dave created the 7 Baby Steps. It's a clear path to know where you are and where you're headed next. This isn't a get-rich-quick scheme, and you haven't won the lottery. But if you follow each step—in order and with great focus and intentionality—you will change your life.

BABY STEP 1
Save $1,000 for Your Starter Emergency Fund

BABY STEP 2
Pay Off All Debt (Except the House) Using the Debt Snowball

BABY STEP 3
Save 3–6 Months of Expenses in a Fully Funded Emergency Fund

BABY STEP 4
Invest 15% of Your Household Income in Retirement

BABY STEP 5
Save for Your Children's College Fund

BABY STEP 6
Pay Off Your Home Early

BABY STEP 7
Build Wealth and Give

COURSE OVERVIEW

You've learned the Baby Steps, but that's not the whole course! You've got nine video lessons ahead of you. The first four will walk you through our proven plan, the 7 Baby Steps. And the last five lessons will teach you how to tackle life on the plan. Let's break it down.

LESSON 01 — BABY STEP 1 & BUDGETING

LESSON 02 — BABY STEP 2

LESSON 03 — BABY STEP 3

LESSON 04 — BABY STEPS 4 5 6 7

The PLAN

Lessons 1–4 walk you through the 7 Baby Steps. This is your proven plan to win with money. In these lessons, you'll learn how to do more than just treat the symptoms of your money problem. You'll get to the root of the problem: your behavior!

LESSON 05 — BUYER BEWARE

LESSON 06 — THE ROLE OF INSURANCE

LESSON 07 — RETIREMENT PLANNING

LESSON 08 — REAL ESTATE & MORTGAGES

LESSON 09 — OUTRAGEOUS GENEROSITY

Life ON THE PLAN

Lessons 5–9 keep you on track with the Baby Steps. Learn to navigate spending, insurance, real estate, and investing, so you don't ruin your progress! And protect yourself from everything trying to get at your money, so you can start fighting for the things you want.

MEET *the* TEAM

Whether you've done stupid with zeros on the end or you're just trying to do a little better, we know that money is a big deal in your life. You may feel ashamed. You may just feel stressed. And if you're not scared, you're probably a little unsure of what to do with your money and where it can take you.

That's why we have a team who's been where you are right now, knows how to win with money, and will help you get there too.

Dave Ramsey, Chris Hogan, and Rachel Cruze are all #1 best-selling authors who speak to sold-out venues across the country. Their books, podcasts, and shows have helped millions of people change their lives. And today, they're going to help you change yours.

DAVE RAMSEY

After battling his way out of bankruptcy and millions of dollars in debt, Dave Ramsey started on a mission to make sure other people discovered the way out. That's why he created *Financial Peace University*. Today, over five million people have experienced life-change through this course. And he's helped millions more through his seven best-selling books, countless live events hosted across the nation, and his radio show, *The Dave Ramsey Show*, heard by more than fifteen million listeners each week. Dave's biblical, commonsense advice is for anyone ready to win with money.

"*Live like no one else*
SO LATER YOU CAN
LIVE AND GIVE LIKE NO ONE ELSE."

Chris HOGAN

While helping clients at a well-respected mortgage company, Chris Hogan felt powerless as he watched people throw away their financial futures. That's when he met Dave Ramsey. For the last decade, Chris has been on our team, on a mission to help millions like you make their money dreams a reality.

Chris is an expert on retirement and wealth building. He's a #1 national best-selling author, dynamic speaker, and financial coach—which means he's seen it all! His newest book is *Everyday Millionaires: How Ordinary People Built Extraordinary Wealth—And How You Can Too*.

"ANYONE IN THIS COUNTRY CAN *become a millionaire.* **I CAN SHOW YOU HOW."**

Rachel CRUZE

Rachel Cruze grew up learning how to win with money. As Dave Ramsey's daughter, she was taught from an early age how to give generously, spend wisely, and save for the future. She understands the dangers of debt, and she's seen firsthand the damage it can do. But as she'll tell you, she's also a spender and hated budgeting until she learned what a budget can really do!

Rachel has authored three best-selling books, is a #1 *New York Times* best-selling author, and is host of *The Rachel Cruze Show*. But what is she most known for? Fun! Rachel is an energetic, personable speaker who wants you to handle your money with wisdom, so you can live a life you love.

"A BUDGET DOESN'T LIMIT YOUR FREEDOM.
A budget gives you freedom."

GETTING *Started*

THANK YOU FOR COORDINATING *FINANCIAL PEACE UNIVERSITY*!

Because of you, people in your community will learn how to take control of their money, and ultimately, change their lives. **You are the heartbeat of this movement.** We couldn't help the millions of people who have been through this course without you!

Whether this is your first time or twentieth time, we're excited to partner with you and walk you step-by-step through leading your class. The next pages will be your tool and your guide. But before you dive in, make sure to identify which type of class you'll be leading: **Traditional or Flex.**

TWO TYPES OF CLASSES

Traditional	These classes watch video lessons together and then go through activities and discussion questions.
Flex	These classes watch the video lessons on their own, but gather to recap the videos and go through activities and discussion questions together.

TRADITIONAL CLASS

If you're scheduled to lead a Traditional Class, you'll meet with your class once a week for nine weeks to work through the entirety of each lesson together. Timed for about 90 minutes, your class will watch the video lesson together, complete the follow-up Activity, answer discussion questions, and review the Action Steps for members to complete before your next class meeting.

Depending on how many people are in your class and how long the Activity and Discussion takes, you may opt for a two-hour class meeting.

If you're leading a Traditional Class, this Coordinator Guide is for you!

FLEX CLASS

When we introduced the online membership, we started offering Flex Classes. This type of class is especially helpful for members and coordinators with busy schedules!

In Flex Classes, members watch the video lessons on their own online at financialpeace.com before coming to the class meeting. Flex Classes usually meet for 45–60 minutes for each lesson, each week. When the class meets, members watch a short recap video of the lesson and move right into the Activity and more discussion questions than the Traditional Class offers. Before the next class meeting, members will complete the Action Steps and watch the next lesson's video.

If you're leading a Flex Class, feel free to flip through this guide to see what a typical lesson format looks like! Then, **download the digital Flex Guide from your Coordinator Dashboard at financialpeace.com.**

LEADING A LARGE CLASS

Whether you're leading a Traditional or Flex Class, we recommend breaking up large classes into **smaller groups of no more than 20 people** for the Discussion portion of the lesson. This will ensure that everyone gets a chance to talk.

When you have multiple smaller groups, you'll need to recruit some help to lead those discussions. That's where a co-coordinator comes in!

YOUR CO-COORDINATOR

A co-coordinator can lead the Discussion for one of the smaller groups and can also help check that each member completed the lesson's Action Steps. Every co-coordinator will need access to your Coordinator Dashboard. (Your Advisor can help you set that up!)

To avoid confusion and potential conflicts, we ask that any communication to your Advisor come through the lead coordinator.

YOU ARE THE *Heartbeat* OF THIS MOVEMENT

YOUR COORDINATOR GUIDE

As both your Coordinator Guide and your Member Workbook, this is the only book you'll need to lead this course every week!

In each lesson, you'll see exactly what your member sees, plus pages just for you. If the page is outlined in yellow (like this one), it's a coordinator-only page. That's where you'll find step-by-step instructions about what to do and what to say in order to lead your class through each lesson.

You'll also notice different icons to quickly indicate what action you should take—whether that's to say specific instructions, start the video, read the discussion questions, or simply wait on your members to finish the Activity.

Don't worry, we'll cover all of this in the next several pages!

Everything You Need to Lead a Class

YOUR COORDINATOR DASHBOARD

In addition to this guide, make sure to use your Coordinator Dashboard at **financialpeace.com**. Everything you need to lead a class is in your dashboard, including a digital version of this guide and contact information for your dedicated Financial Peace advisor!

You'll see references to your Coordinator Dashboard throughout this guide for things like taking attendance, messaging your class, recording your class's Financial Snapshot figures, and even starting your next class! Your dashboard is the best place to communicate with and keep up with your members. Plus, if you need to access the online member experience, you can do that too.

From your dashboard, you'll also have access to the online Coordinator Store, and you'll find all the incredible perks you get as one of our amazing coordinators!

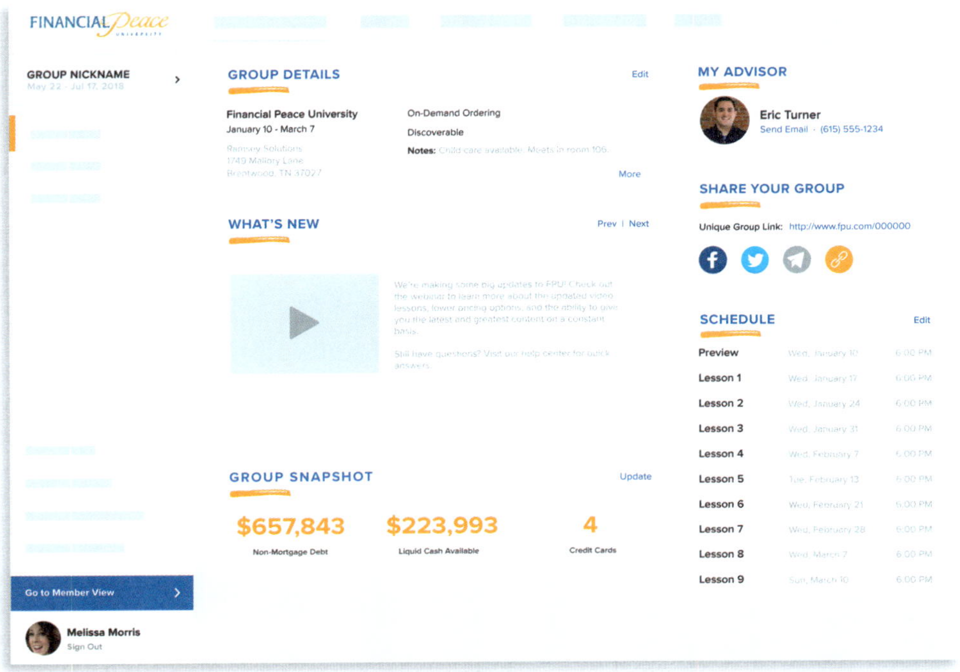

COORDINATOR *Perks*

As a thank you for everything you do, and mostly for helping us change lives, we have perks—just for you!

You get all the member perks too!

THE *Support* YOU NEED

- A Financial Peace Membership for every year you coordinate (which means, you get all of the member perks listed on the next page)
- An online community of other coordinators through your Coordinator Dashboard
- Exclusive access to coordinatorcentral.com with special pricing on materials for your class and discounts on other Ramsey Solutions products just for you

THE *Impact* YOU MAKE

- Based on the attendance you track each week and the information you'll receive from the Financial Snapshot cards in Lessons 2 and 9, you'll be able to see the incredible impact you've had on your class. My Impact shows you the total debt paid off, money saved, credit cards cut up, and other stats for your class (and every class you lead!).

MEMBER *Perks*

Members get access to financialpeace.com which includes:

THE *Knowledge* THEY NEED

- *Financial Peace University*
- *The Legacy Journey* course
- *Smart Money Smart Kids* course

THE *Tools* TO GET THERE

- EveryDollar Plus
- Emergency Fund Planner, Debt Snowball Tool, Investment Calculator, and more
- Endorsed Local Providers and SmartVestor Pros
- Ramsey Preferred Coaches

THE *Community* TO HELP

- Financial Peace online community
- Access to any *Financial Peace University* class, nationwide

FINANCIAL PEACE *Membership*

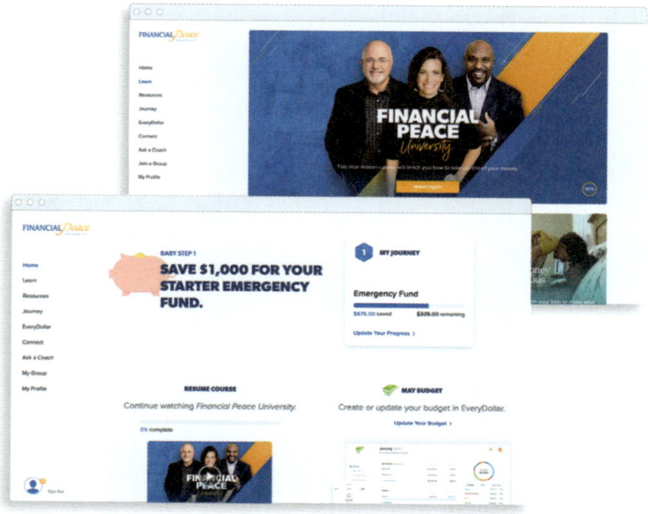

All the incredible resources that are available to your members are also available to you! To access the online member experience, just click "Go to Member View" in the side navigation of your dashboard.

Familiarizing yourself with the member experience will help you feel more confident answering questions in class. Plus, it's the best resource to help you on your own journey to financial peace!

SET UP EVERYDOLLAR

Once you're signed in to your financialpeace.com account, it's time to start your EveryDollar membership.

1. Click EveryDollar in the navigation on financialpeace.com.
2. Click Sign In to EveryDollar.
3. Sign in using your financialpeace.com email and password.
4. Connect your bank to easily track transactions!

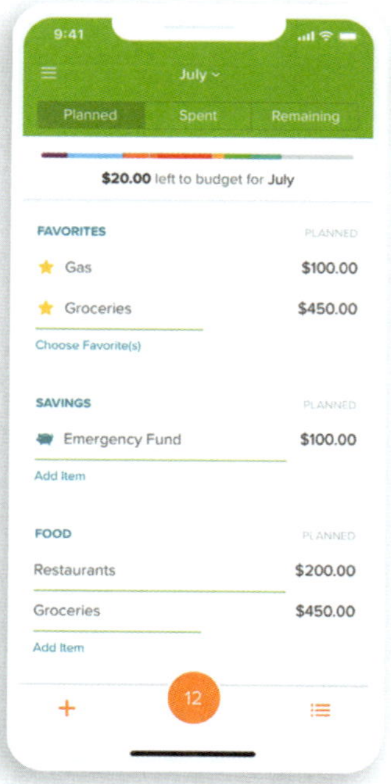

We've GOT YOUR BACK!

No matter what questions you or your members have, our team is available to help you get the answers and solutions you need to lead your class with confidence!

YOUR ADVISOR

Your dedicated Financial Peace advisor is your primary, trusted contact. Reach out to them if you need to order materials for your class, if you want more tips on promoting your class, or if you just want to share an amazing story of life-change from your class!

You can find the name of your advisor and their contact information on the Coordinator Dashboard.

THE COORDINATOR SUPPORT TEAM

This team is all about making sure you feel confident leading your class and have an amazing coordinator experience! The Coordinator Support team can answer questions about what you can expect during a class and can help you update class details or solve any issues in your class.

Email coordinatorhelp@financialpeace.com or call 877.378.2667 opt. 2.

THE CUSTOMER SUCCESS TEAM

These are our digital product experts. The Customer Success team can help you or your members navigate and troubleshoot financialpeace.com and EveryDollar. If you want to find answers on your own, check out our up-to-date, extensive Help Center (help.financialpeace.com).

Email help@financialpeace.com or call 877.378.2667 opt. 1.

4 PARTS to Leading a CLASS

Now, let's look at what coordinating *Financial Peace University* actually looks like! Leading a class is broken down into four easy-to-follow parts. We've given you a quick description on the next page, but we'll tell you everything you need to know in the next few pages.

1 PROMOTE
& PREP

Before you can lead a class, you need a class to lead! Spread the word about your class in order to get as many member sign-ups as possible! After you have your class ready, we'll help you prepare for your very first meeting.

2 BEFORE
EACH LESSON

There are a few simple steps you'll follow before you meet each week. We'll walk you through how to prepare for the upcoming lesson and how to set up the meeting room for your class.

3 DURING
EACH LESSON

Each lesson follows the same format: Introduction, Video, Activity, Discussion, Action Steps, and a Deep Dive. Remember, we'll give you specific instructions that will walk you through what to say and what to do.

4 AFTER
EACH LESSON

There are specific steps you'll need to take after you've dismissed your class and before the next lesson—things like updating attendance and messaging your class.

1 PROMOTE & PREP

Promote

Promotion is just a personal invitation from you to someone who may need *Financial Peace University*. The more people you invite to join your class, the more lives you'll help change!

Your Advisor will be mailing you, or has already mailed you, a Starter Guide. This pack will walk you through how and when to promote your class—and provide you with posters and resources so you can start as soon as possible! But we'll give you one piece of advice right now: **It's not so much *how* you promote, but how *often* you promote.**

On your Coordinator Dashboard, you'll find even more promotion resources (like posters, videos, and social media images and sample text), a full promotion timeline, plus the most important tool you have: **your unique class link**. From this page, people can purchase memberships, sign up for your class, or ask you questions about your class. Be sure to include this link on *all* of your promotion materials!

Take a minute to find it on your dashboard and write it below.

YOUR UNIQUE CLASS LINK

Prep

Your first class sets the tone for the entire course. It's a big deal! Spend some extra time preparing for your first class.

- ☐ **Help people purchase a membership and join your class.**

Prep: One Week Before

- ☐ **Contact volunteers.**
  Reach out to any volunteers, childcare helpers, and co-coordinators to make sure they'll be ready for your first class.

- ☐ **Watch Lesson 1 and work through the Activity.**

- ☐ **Post last-call promotions!**
  Post one more time on social media for final group sign-ups. Don't forget to include your unique class link!

- ☐ **Message registered class members.**
  Using the message feature on your Coordinator Dashboard, send a message to all registered members. Introduce yourself and remind them of your class details (time, start date, and location).

Promotional posters are in your Starter Guide.

2 BEFORE EACH LESSON

Come back to these checklists and mark off each box before every lesson. If a lesson requires anything beyond what is listed here, we'll let you know in the Lesson Prep section at the beginning of that lesson.

Before Your Class Meets

- ☐ **Watch each lesson video.**
  You can watch lesson videos from your DVDs or on financialpeace.com. From the class schedule listed on your Coordinator Dashboard, select each lesson title to go straight to the video you need to watch next.

- ☐ **Complete each lesson Activity and review the discussion questions.**
  Review the lesson before your class members so you can help answer questions that might come up. But remember, "I don't know" is a totally acceptable answer! You can always direct members to the Ask a Coach feature on their Financial Peace online membership or team up with your Advisor later to get answers to any questions you can't answer.

- ☐ **Pray for a great lesson!**
  God is at the center of this course, and ultimately, He's the one who will reshape the hearts and minds of everyone in your class! Pray for a great class and for each of your members by name.

At Your Meeting Space

- ☐ **Unlock the doors** and hang any signs needed to direct people to the meeting location.
- ☐ **Bring this guide, extra pens and pencils**, and any additional items as noted in the Lesson Prep section at the beginning of each lesson.
- ☐ **Check the audio and visual equipment,** including volume levels—be prepared to play the video with either your DVDs or by streaming on financialpeace.com.
- ☐ **Arrange the tables and chairs** for video viewing and class discussion.
- ☐ **Welcome everyone** as they arrive. Try to greet them by name!

Be Sure to Bring

Coordinator Guide

DVD Player

DVD

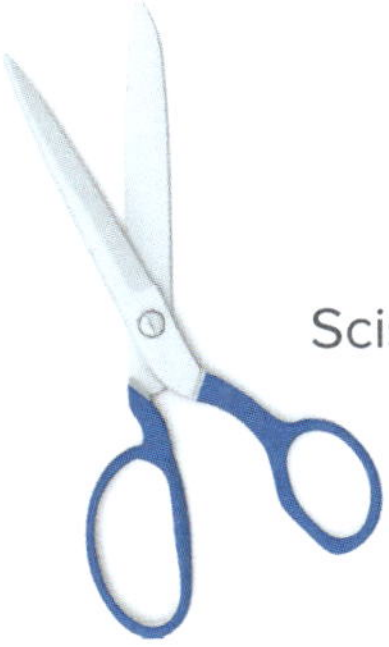

Scissors

Extra Pens & Pencils

3 DURING EACH LESSON

Each lesson follows the same format. Look for your yellow, coordinator-only pages throughout the lesson. These will tell you exactly what to do and what to say to your members.

BEFORE THE VIDEO STARTS

START THE LESSON

After you welcome members to your meeting space, you're ready to start leading your class through the beginning of the lesson, before you play the video.

Any time you see the yellow border, it's a coordinator page!

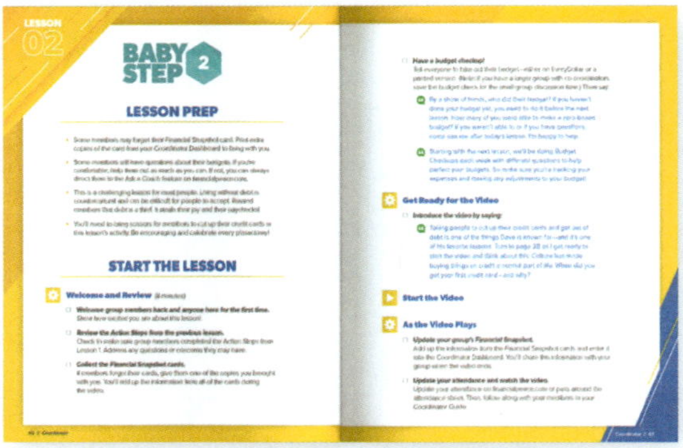

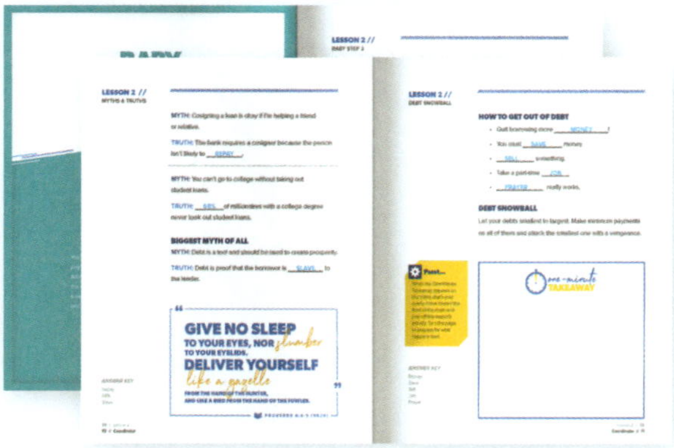

AS THE VIDEO PLAYS

FOLLOW ALONG

Then look for your coordinator cue near the One-Minute Takeaway at the end of the fill in the blanks. This is your reminder to transition to the Activity.

WHEN THE VIDEO ENDS

ACTIVITY

Each lesson has at least one activity that you'll go through as a class after the video ends. Remember, your yellow, coordinator-only page will walk you step-by-step through leading the Activity.

Do these right after the video!

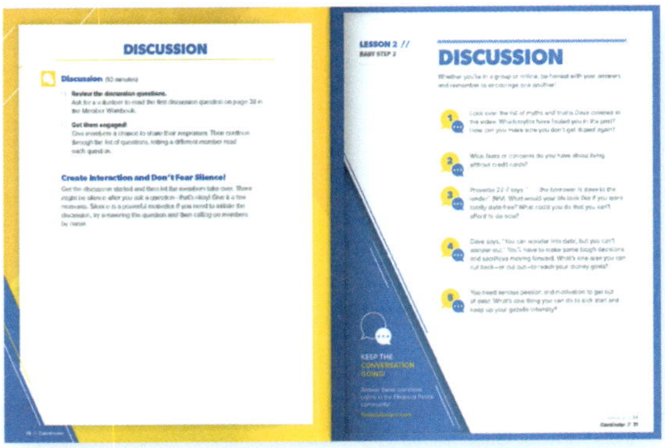

DISCUSSION

After the Activity, you'll move on to the discussion questions. These are specific to each lesson! Make sure to allow time for your class to talk about each question.

This page is what your class sees!

ENDING THE LESSON

Before dismissing your class, you'll review the Action Steps your members need to complete before the next lesson. Then, just wrap up and clean up!

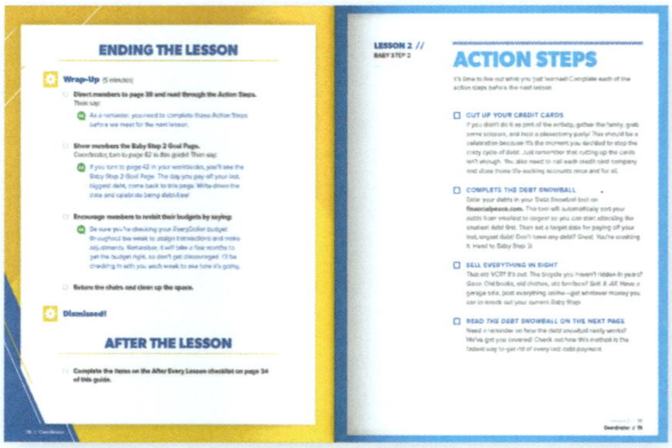

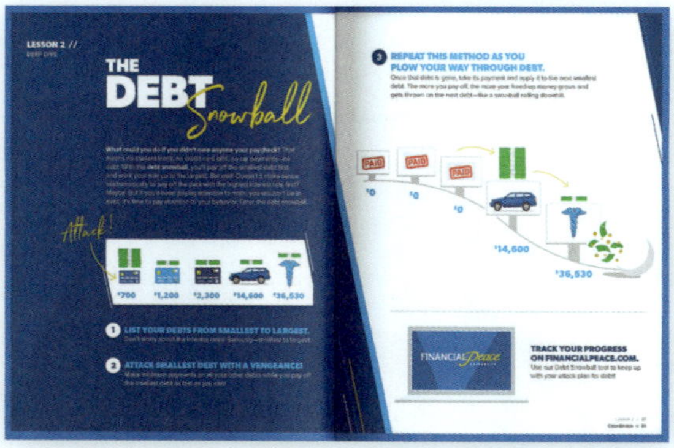

Deep Dives are made for members to read on their own, before the next lesson.

COORDINATOR CUES

On each of your yellow, coordinator-only pages, look out for these icons to quickly see what to say and what to do. Yep, it's that easy.

- *Say this out loud to your class.*
- *Complete a task or take an action.*
- *Lead your class through the Activity.*
- *Lead your class through the Discussion.*

22 // Lesson 1
52 // Coordinator

On some pages, you will see two page numbers: your Coordinator Guide page number and the corresponding page number in the Member Workbook.

REMINDERS DURING EACH LESSON

- ☐ **Follow your Coordinator Guide to lead your class through each lesson.** From introducing them to the lesson to reviewing the Action Steps they'll need to complete before the next lesson, we've got you covered.

- ☐ **At the start of every lesson, be sure to take attendance.** You can do this right in your Coordinator Dashboard. If you're more of a pen-and-paper person, you can also print out attendance sheets from your dashboard. It's important that your members understand the importance of working through the lessons together as a class!

Take attendance online or print out sheets from your dashboard.

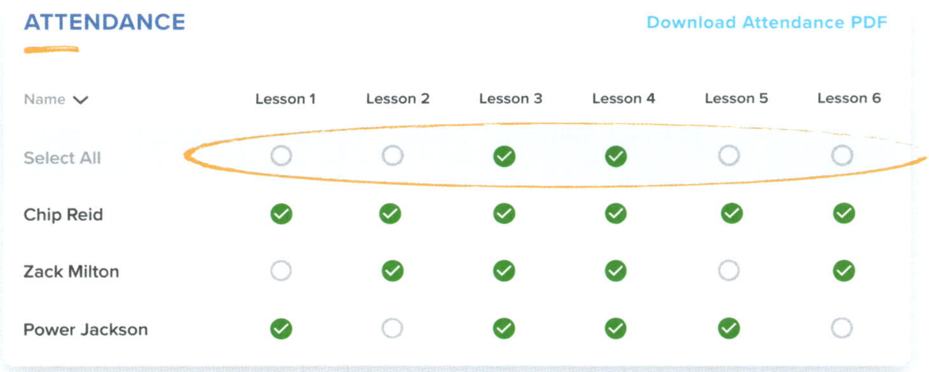

- ☐ **Collect Financial Snapshot cards from your members at the start of Lessons 2 and 9. (We'll remind you of this in the lessons.)** You'll then need to transfer that information to the Financial Snapshot feature in your Coordinator Dashboard. This is incredible information to share with class members and the leadership at your meeting space to help promote future classes.

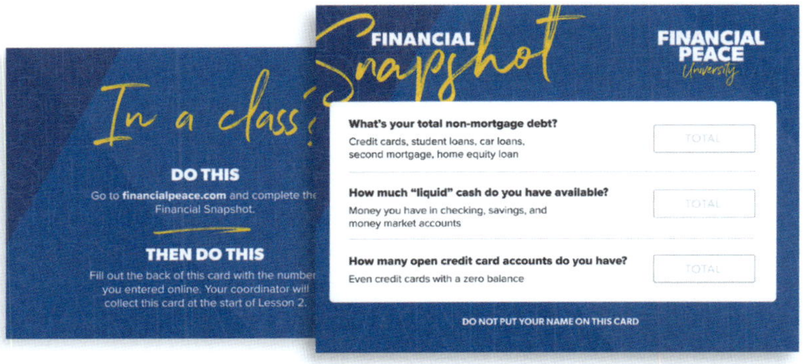

Lesson 2 and 9 cards are slightly different.

Tips FOR A GREAT LESSON

Behavior change happens when people sit face-to-face and work through their hopes, dreams, and fears about money together. That's why it's so important to create the right environment for your class. Remember, your job is not to "fix" your class members. Your job is to provide hope.

Make It a Safe Place

When someone joins a class, they're often stepping far outside their comfort zone. In fact, we've found that many people walk into their first class with a strong sense of guilt, shame, or fear about their personal financial situation. Let them know that's okay! We've all messed up, and we've all done dumb things with money. Encourage your class members—cheer them on for making the hard decision to change their lives.

Encourage Openness and Excitement

Everyone in the room will take their cue from you—so if you open up, listen intently to others, and use humor and personal stories, the rest of the class will too! Don't be afraid to share your own stories of messing up with money and how *Financial Peace University* has helped you.

Create Interaction

Get the discussion started and then let the members take over. The best classes are the ones in which members hold each other accountable. And remember, if you don't know the answer to a question, "I don't know" is a totally acceptable response! Then, feel free to reach out to your Advisor for the answer or direct members to the Ask a Coach feature on their Financial Peace online membership.

Don't Fear Silence

Sometimes there will be silence after you ask a question. That's okay! Give it a few moments. Silence is a powerful motivator.

Remind Members to Use the Membership

Encourage class members to take full advantage of their membership. While the class creates accountability and motivation, the tools and resources on financialpeace.com will help them put what they're learning into practice. Encourage members to engage with their online membership to help them reach financial peace even faster!

4 AFTER EACH LESSON

After you've dismissed your class at the end of each lesson, there are specific things you'll need to do before the next lesson. Complete the following checklist to stay connected with your class members and keep up with your coordinator duties. Make sure to do this after every single lesson.

What to Do

- [ ] **Update class attendance.**
  You'll keep track of weekly attendance right in your Coordinator Dashboard (don't miss the Select All feature). If you print out an attendance sheet to use during the video, make sure to enter the information online after each lesson.

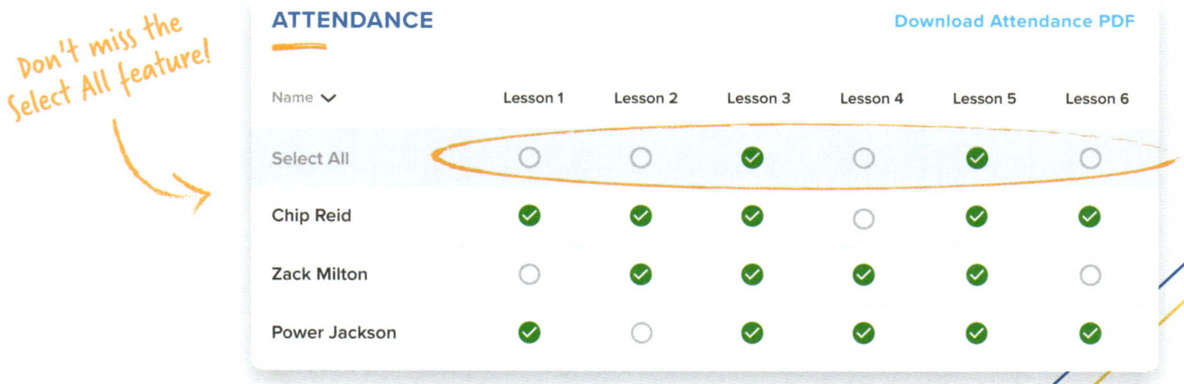

- [ ] **Message your class.**
The messaging feature in your Coordinator Dashboard allows you to send a message to your class members—both attendees and absentees. You can use the templates with suggested messages for each lesson to make this step quick and easy! But we encourage you to read over each template and add some personality to your message.

Check out the message templates.

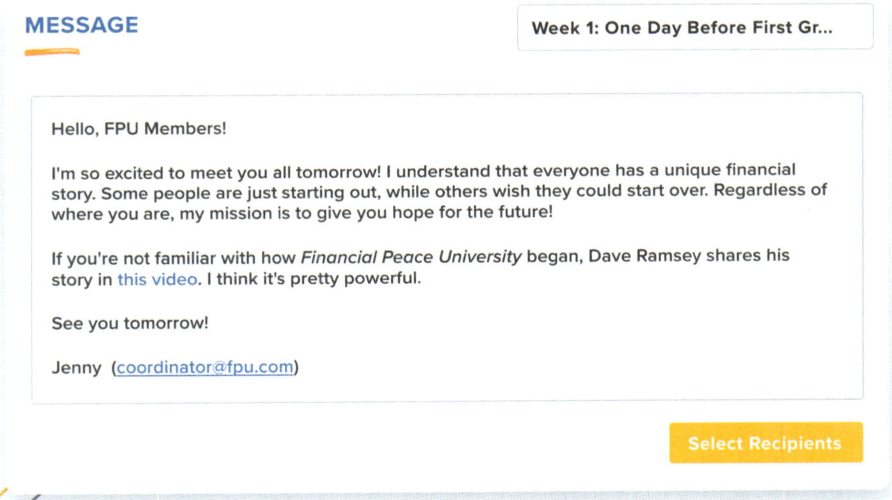

- [ ] **Pray for each of your class members.**
If you haven't noticed, we want to make sure God is at the center of this whole course! Take time before and after each lesson to pray for every single member of your class.

- [ ] **Complete the Action Steps.**
Whatever your class members do, you should do as well! To best help them, we want you to understand each and every lesson. Plus, if you're working through the Baby Steps, these Action Steps will help you on your *own* plan.

Ready?

IT'S GAME ON!

BABY STEP 1 & BUDGETING

LESSON PREP

- You may have people who haven't registered for your class or need to buy materials. Be ready to help them before they leave.
- Bring extra workbooks (if you have them) or print copies of Lesson 1 from your Coordinator Dashboard.
- People will be attending your class for a lot of different reasons. Create a comfortable and welcoming place for them to open up and tackle their problems head on.
- Budgeting isn't always people's favorite topic, but it's the foundation of this course and critical to their success with money! Make sure you've set up your own EveryDollar account so you're familiar with it and can help members.

START THE LESSON

Welcome (10 minutes)

- ☐ **Introduce yourself and your co-coordinator (if you have one).** Describe your experience with FPU, talk about classes you've led (if any), and share your excitement about coordinating this class. Then say:

  Welcome to *Financial Peace University*! I'm so excited that you decided to join this class. This nine-lesson course will help you change the way you think about and handle money. Each lesson will follow the same format. We'll watch a video and complete an Activity. Then, after some Discussion, we'll review the Action Steps you'll need to complete before we meet for the next lesson.

- ☐ **Ask members to introduce themselves.**

  Everyone take about 30 seconds to introduce yourself. Tell us your name and why you decided to attend *Financial Peace University*.

- ☐ **Encourage members to attend each lesson by saying:**

  The reason we go through the lessons together is so we can encourage and learn from each other. In order to graduate from this course, you'll need to attend at least eight lessons! But if you do miss one, just make sure you work through that lesson on financialpeace.com.

- ☐ **Take care of housekeeping.** Make sure to point out where the restrooms are located, explain any changes in meeting dates, and ask that they silence their cell phones.

Get Ready for the Video

- ☐ **Instruct everyone to turn to page 15 in their Member Workbook.**
- ☐ **Introduce the video by saying:**

  > As we watch the video, you'll see keywords at the bottom of the screen. Write those words in the blanks in your workbook. Before I start the video, think about this: What would you do if you had a $1,000 emergency tomorrow?

Start the Video

As the Video Plays

- ☐ **Update your attendance and watch the video.**
  Update attendance on your Coordinator Dashboard or pass around the FPU Attendance Sheet and then update it online after the lesson. The next pages match the Member Workbook so you can follow along with the video.
- ☐ **Look for your coordinator cue before the One-Minute Takeaway to get ready for the Activity.**

LESSON 01

"A BUDGET IS **PERMISSION** to *spend.*"

—RACHEL CRUZE

BABY STEP 1 & BUDGETING

KEY POINTS

The 7 Baby Steps focus on changing your behavior toward money through a proven, step-by-step plan.

Baby Step 1 is saving $1,000 for your starter emergency fund.

A zero-based budget is the tool that helps you take control of your money.

BABY STEP

1

Save $1,000 for Your Starter Emergency Fund

Your first goal is to save $1,000 for your starter emergency fund as fast as you possibly can. Saving has to become a priority. Focus all of your energy on getting this Baby Step done—fast! An emergency is going to happen, so you have to be ready when it hits. We're talking no credit cards, but real cash in the bank to cover it.

THE 7 BABY STEPS

GUIDE
Dave Ramsey

BABY STEP 1

Save __$1,000__ for your starter emergency fund.

If you will live like no one else now, later you can live and __GIVE__ like no one else.

> **NO DISCIPLINE SEEMS PLEASANT**
> **AT THE TIME, BUT PAINFUL. LATER ON, HOWEVER, IT PRODUCES A**
> *harvest of righteousness and peace*
> **FOR THOSE WHO HAVE BEEN TRAINED BY IT.**
>
> HEBREWS 12:11 (NIV)

GUIDE
Rachel Cruze

BUDGETING

Give it __THREE__ __MONTHS__ to get into a rhythm.

The __NERD__ enjoys doing the budget.

The __FREE__ __SPIRIT__ feels controlled by the budget.

ANSWER KEY

$1,000
Give
Three Months
Nerd
Free Spirit

In the Budget Committee ____**MEETING**____, you will meet with your spouse to review the next month's budget.

The budget gives you ____**CONTROL**____ you never knew you had.

> "SUPPOSE ONE OF YOU WANTS TO BUILD A TOWER. **WON'T YOU FIRST SIT DOWN AND ESTIMATE THE COST** TO SEE IF YOU HAVE ENOUGH MONEY TO *complete it?*"
>
> LUKE 14:28 (NIV)

Notes

ANSWER KEY

Meeting
Control

It must be a zero-based budget. That means your income minus expenses equals ___**ZERO**___.

The ___**FOUR**___ ___**WALLS**___ are food, utilities, shelter, and transportation.

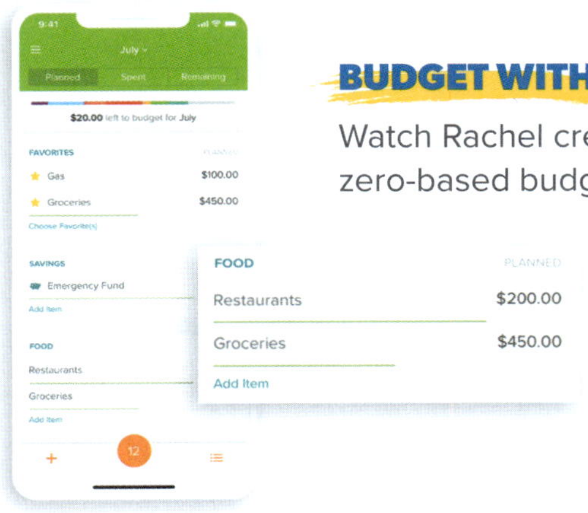

BUDGET WITH EVERYDOLLAR

Watch Rachel create a sample zero-based budget!

Pssst...

When the One-Minute Takeaway appears on the video, that's your cue to move toward the front of the room and kick off this lesson's Activity. Turn the page to prepare for what happens next.

one-minute TAKEAWAY

ANSWER KEY

Zero
Four Walls

ACTIVITIES

When the Video Ends

- ☐ **After the One-Minute Takeaway, say:**

  We just heard a lot of information. That was a lot to take in! So now we're going to do some activities that will help you create your first budget.

Activity: Nerd & Free Spirit Quiz (4 minutes)

- ☐ **Introduce the Nerd & Free Spirit Quiz on page 18 by saying:**

  For the first Activity, let's turn to page 18 in your workbooks. Can I get a volunteer to read "What to Do" for the Nerd & Free Spirit Quiz?

- ☐ **Wait for the volunteer to finish reading, then say:**

  This quiz isn't an exact science—it's meant to be fun! If your spouse is with you, make sure you take the quiz together on the same sheet. Spend a few minutes working through the quiz now.

- ☐ **Allow time for members to complete the Activity, then say:**

  If you're a Nerd, raise your hand. If you're a Free Spirit, raise your hand. Some of you may have a little of both, but generally, you'll lean one way or the other.

  What surprised you about the results of your quiz?

  Now that you know your personality, you can see what your role is in the Budget Committee Meeting.

Activity: Budget Committee Rules (1 minute)

- ☐ **Read the Budget Committee Meeting rules by saying:**

> In the video, Rachel covered three main rules for a Budget Committee Meeting to work. Let's take a look at those now. Can I get a Nerd to read the Free Spirit rules out loud? And will a Free Spirit read the Nerd rules?

Activity: Quick-Start Budget (7 minutes)

- ☐ **Introduce the Quick-Start Budget on page 20 by saying:**

> Now that you know your money personality and understand the rules of the Budget Committee Meeting, it's time to do your Quick-Start Budget.
>
> This is just a warm-up for the EveryDollar budget you'll do later. It won't be super detailed. The idea is to start seeing how you're spending your money. Now, turn to page 20 and take a few minutes to fill out your Quick-Start Budget.

- ☐ **Allow time for members to complete the Activity, then say:**

> Keep in mind, these activities will help you build an EveryDollar budget that will allow you to plan for every single dollar you bring in for the month. If you need help budgeting for an irregular income or week by week, there are example forms on pages 142–147 of your workbook.

Note: If you're comfortable, offer budgeting guidance before you dismiss your class.

When the Activity Ends

- ☐ **Turn to page 54 of this guide for instructions on how to lead your class through the discussion questions.**

LESSON 1 //
ACTIVITY

NERD & *Free Spirit* QUIZ

WHAT TO DO:

Take this fun quiz to figure out if you're more of a Nerd or a Free Spirit! If you're married, this will help you identify your role in the Budget Committee Meeting. If you're single, this will help you determine your strengths in creating your budget, and where you'll need some accountability.

PICK THE ONE THAT SOUNDS MOST LIKE YOU!

PERSON 1 A	PERSON 1 B		PERSON 2 A	PERSON 2 B
○	○	A: You're prepared for Tax Day months in advance. *B: Tax Day? That's in October, right?*	○	○
○	○	A: Rules are important and should always be followed. *B: Rules are more like suggestions.*	○	○
○	○	A: You are always on time. Always. *B: You show up "on time," give or take 15 minutes.*	○	○
○	○	A: You make a plan for each day of your vacation. *B: Vacations are more fun with no schedule.*	○	○
○	○	A: You read the introductions of books. They're in there for a reason! *B: You skip introductions—only chapters count.*	○	○
○	○	A: Your life's motto: "A place for everything and everything in its place." *B: You live by the phrase, "It'll all work out!"*	○	○
○	○	A: You organize your shirts by color. Doesn't everyone? *B: You're doing good just to get your shirts off the floor.*	○	○
○	○	A: You can't wait to create your EveryDollar budget! *B: You're considering faking an illness for the Budget Committee Meeting.*	○	○
☐ A	☐ B	← **TOTAL YOUR SCORES AND CIRCLE THE HIGHEST ONE** →	☐ A	☐ B

IF YOU HAD A HIGH SCORE OF: A

SCORE

4–5: **NERD-ISH**
You have a pretty good idea of how much money is in your account.

6–7: **NERD**
Budgets are for awesome people.

8: **ULTRA NERD**
You canceled your plans with friends so you could start drafting next month's budget.

IF YOU HAD A HIGH SCORE OF: B

SCORE

4–5: **FREE SPIRIT-ISH**
You've got a budget somewhere. You could find it if you needed to.

6–7: **FREE SPIRIT**
Budgets are for boring people.

8: **ULTRA FREE SPIRIT**
Budgets are like putting on a straitjacket. Why would you ever do that to yourself?

OFFICIAL RULES OF THE BUDGET COMMITTEE MEETING

FOR THE NERD

1. Create the budget.
2. Thank the Free Spirit for being there!
3. Show the budget to the Free Spirit. Then be quiet.

FOR THE FREE SPIRIT

1. Come to the Budget Committee Meeting.
2. Be realistic and don't use the phrase "whatever you think."
3. Have an opinion and change something.

LESSON 1 //
ACTIVITY

WHAT TO DO:

Fill out your estimated monthly expenses for the following categories. Then add up the total for all categories.

SEE WHAT YOU'RE *Spending*

Now that you know whether you're more of a Nerd or a Free Spirit, it's time to take the first step into budgeting. Don't panic; this first step is simple!

THE BUDGET IS YOUR MAP FOR THE MONTH

Rachel taught you how to create a zero-based budget with EveryDollar. But to get to where you want to go, you have to know where you are.

It's just like driving: if you don't know your starting point, it's impossible to get to your destination! That's why you do a **Quick-Start Budget.**

IT'S TIME TO FILL OUT THE QUICK-START BUDGET

This activity is a simple way to put pen to paper and get you thinking about how much you're currently spending in each category, each month. You'll notice there are a few categories missing, like income and debt. That's okay! Remember, this is just your starting point.

Free Spirits, make sure there is fun in the budget!

Nerds, this is where you get to work with numbers!

☐ **STEP 1**

Write down what you're spending for the month in each item of each category. If you don't know exact numbers, just make your best guess!

☐ **STEP 2**

Add up each item in each category and write the TOTAL at the bottom.

☐ **STEP 3**

Add up the numbers in all of the TOTAL boxes and write that number in the TOTAL FOR CATEGORIES box.

YOUR QUICK-START BUDGET

Follow Steps 1–3 on the previous page to list and add up your monthly expenses.

GIVING	Planned
Church	
Charity	
TOTAL	

FOOD	Planned
Groceries	
Restaurants	
TOTAL	

PERSONAL	Planned
Clothing	
Phone	
Fun Money	
Gifts	
TOTAL	

TRANSPORTATION	Planned
Auto Insurance	
Gas & Oil	
Maintenance	
TOTAL	

HOUSING	Planned
Mortgage/Rent	
Utilities	
TOTAL	

TOTAL FOR CATEGORIES	

Remember, this total does not include every category that will be in your monthly budget—just a few of the big ones!

Great Start!

You've taken the first step to creating your monthly budget. In the Action Steps, you'll **create a zero-based budget with EveryDollar—just like Rachel showed you!**

DISCUSSION

Discussion (8 minutes)

- ☐ **Introduce the Discussion by saying:**

  In every lesson, we'll go through a list of questions that will allow us to dig deeper into the principles we learned in the video. We're going to read a question together and then take some time to discuss before we move on to the next question. Let's turn to page 22 in your workbooks. Can I get a volunteer to read the first question?

- ☐ **Get them engaged!**
  Give members a chance to share their responses. Then continue through the list of questions, letting a different member read each question.

Create Interaction and Don't Fear Silence!

Get the discussion started and then let the members take over. There might be silence after you ask a question—that's okay! Give it a few moments. Silence is a powerful motivator. If you need to initiate the discussion, try answering the question and then calling on members by name.

DISCUSSION

This is where change happens—in a safe space where you can talk about real life. This is where you *start* connecting with other people and *stop* believing you're in this alone. Whether you're in a class or online, be honest with your answers and remember to encourage the people around you!

1. Think about a time when an emergency stressed you out. How would a starter emergency fund have made that a *stress-free* emergency?

2. What are some categories that you think might bust your budget? What can you do to keep those categories under control?

3. Cashing out your budget can help you stay ahead of problem categories. Which categories could you use envelopes or clips for to help you stick to your budget?

4. Based on your results from the Nerd & Free Spirit Quiz, what strengths can you bring to the Budget Committee Meeting?

KEEP THE CONVERSATION GOING!

Answer these questions online in the Financial Peace community!

financialpeace.com

ENDING THE LESSON

Wrap-Up (5 minutes)

- ☐ **Introduce and read through the Action Steps by saying:**

  Let's move on to the Action Steps on page 23. You'll need to complete these before we meet for the next lesson. Let's read through them now.

- ☐ **Ask for a volunteer to read the Baby Step 1 Goal on page 26.** Coordinator, turn to page 60 in this guide!

- ☐ **Encourage them to bring their budget to the next lesson by saying:**

  Make sure you bring your EveryDollar budget with you to the next lesson—this can be on your phone or a printout. No one will look at the exact numbers, but one of my jobs every week is to do a budget checkup.

- ☐ **Highlight the Financial Peace Membership benefits by saying:**

  There are a ton of tools and resources you'll need to use throughout this course, so make sure to set up your financialpeace.com account if you haven't yet.

- ☐ **Invite anyone who has not yet registered or purchased class materials to stay after the lesson.**

- ☐ **Return the chairs and clean up the space.**

Dismissed!

AFTER THE LESSON

- ☐ **Complete the items on the After Each Lesson checklist on pages 36–37 of this guide.**

In a class?

DO THIS

Go to **financialpeace.com** and complete the Financial Snapshot.

THEN DO THIS

Fill out the back of this card with the numbers you entered online. Your coordinator will collect this card at the start of Lesson 2.

FINANCIAL *Snapshot*

FINANCIAL PEACE *University*

What's your total non-mortgage debt?

Credit cards, student loans, car loans, second mortgage, home equity loan

TOTAL

How much "liquid" cash do you have available?

Money you have in checking, savings, and money market accounts

TOTAL

How many open credit card accounts do you have?

Even credit cards with a zero balance

TOTAL

DO NOT PUT YOUR NAME ON THIS CARD

ACTION STEPS

Personal finance is 80% behavior. It's only 20% head knowledge. So it's time to live out what you just learned! Complete each of the Action Steps before the next lesson. (If you're married, do this with your spouse.) You got this!

- ☐ **KNOCK OUT BABY STEP 1**
  It's time to draw a line in the sand! This is when you decide to change. Head over to **financialpeace.com** and identify which Baby Step you're on! If you're on Baby Step 1, use the Emergency Fund Planner to get $1,000 in the bank as fast as you can. If you've already got your $1,000, well done! Move on to the next Action Step.

- ☐ **CREATE A BUDGET WITH EVERYDOLLAR**
  Your Quick-Start Budget was a great way to get the hang of budgeting. Now, create a zero-based budget with **EveryDollar.** Married couples, don't forget the Budget Committee Meeting. And singles, show your budget to your accountability partner and ask for feedback. If you have an irregular income or want to budget weekly, use the Irregular Income or Allocated Spending forms on **financialpeace.com**. Examples of these forms are on pages 140–145.

- ☐ **COMPLETE YOUR FINANCIAL SNAPSHOT**
  Use the Financial Snapshot tool at **financialpeace.com** to list your debt, savings, and active credit cards. If you're in a class, transfer that information to the Financial Snapshot card (page 24) and turn it in to your coordinator at the start of Lesson 2.

- ☐ **READ *THE POWERFUL ZERO-BASED BUDGET* ON THE NEXT PAGE**
  The only way to control your money is with a budget—a zero-based budget. Want a quick refresher on how to easily make one with EveryDollar? Read on!

THE *Powerful* ZERO-BASED BUDGET

Whether you're on Baby Step 1 or 7, you need a budget. It's your map for every month. And it puts you in control of your money.

Want to pay off debt? *You need a budget.* Want to build your emergency fund? *You need a budget.* Already investing? You're not off the hook—*you still need a budget.* And not just any budget—that's right, a zero-based budget.

A zero-based budget simply means your income minus your expenses equals zero. One more time: Your income minus *everything else* equals zero. That means you give every dollar a job to do—every month. *Hint: That's why we named our tool EveryDollar.* Plan on purpose for every dollar, every month!

1. **START WITH YOUR INCOME**
2. **LIST ALL YOUR EXPENSES**
3. **SUBTRACT EXPENSES FROM INCOME**
4. **TRACK YOUR EXPENSES**
5. **BE FLEXIBLE!**

HOW TO DO A MONTHLY BUDGET

1 START WITH YOUR INCOME

Write down all the income you expect for the month.

INCOME	
Paycheck	$3,500

2 LIST ALL YOUR EXPENSES

Remember what Rachel said: This is *everything* under income, from giving to miscellaneous!

EXPENSES	
Giving	$350
Saving	$450
Rent	$875
Utilities	$350
Groceries/Restaurants	$525
Transportation	$350
Insurance	$500
Miscellaneous	$100

3 SUBTRACT EXPENSES FROM INCOME

If your income minus your expenses equals zero, you did it! You've just made a zero-based budget. If it doesn't, you've got some work to do! Adjust some categories and get to zero.

	INCOME
–	EXPENSES
=	$0

4 TRACK YOUR EXPENSES

Track your expenses every day during the month to make sure you're sticking to your budget. If you're overspending, make adjustments in your categories and then learn to say no!

5 BE FLEXIBLE!

Planning for payments shows you just how much debt steals your income! Let's say you have a car payment of $325 and a student loan payment of $150. You need to include those debts in your budget and adjust other categories to account for those expenses. Remember, your income minus *everything else* has to equal zero.

DEBTS	
Car Payment	$325
Student Loan	$150

EXPENSES	
Saving	$200
Groceries/Restaurants	$300

Updated Totals

BABY STEP 1

As soon as you get $1,000 in the bank, come back to this page and mark the date you officially knocked out Baby Step 1!

GOAL

$1,000

DATE COMPLETED

_____ / _____ / _____

MONTH DAY YEAR

This is the
EASIEST
and the
HARDEST STEP.

LESSON 02

BABY STEP 2

LESSON PREP

- Some members may forget their Financial Snapshot card. Print extra copies of the card from your Coordinator Dashboard to bring with you.
- Some members will have questions about their budgets. If you're comfortable, help them out as much as you can. If not, you can always direct them to the Ask a Coach feature on financialpeace.com.
- This is a challenging lesson for most people. Living without debt is countercultural and can be difficult for people to accept. Remind members that debt is a thief. It steals their joy and their paychecks!
- You'll need to bring scissors for members to cut up their credit cards in this lesson's Activity. Be encouraging and celebrate every plasectomy!

START THE LESSON

Welcome and Review (8 minutes)

- ☐ **Welcome class members back and anyone here for the first time.** Show how excited you are about this lesson!
- ☐ **Review the Action Steps from the previous lesson.** Check to make sure class members completed the Action Steps from Lesson 1. Address any questions or concerns they may have.
- ☐ **Collect the Financial Snapshot cards.** If members forgot their cards, give them one of the copies you brought with you. You'll add up the information from all of the cards during the video.

- [ ] **Have a budget checkup!**
Tell everyone to take out their budget—either on EveryDollar or a printed version. (Note: If you have a larger class with co-coordinators, save the budget check for the small-group discussion time.) Then say:

> By a show of hands, who did their budget? If you haven't done your budget yet, you need to do it before the next lesson. How many of you were able to make a zero-based budget? If you weren't able to or if you have questions, come see me after today's lesson. I'm happy to help.

> Starting with the next lesson, we'll be doing budget checkups each week with different questions to help perfect your budgets. So make sure you're tracking your expenses and making any adjustments to your categories!

Get Ready for the Video

- [ ] **Introduce the video by saying:**

> Telling people to cut up their credit cards and get out of debt is one of the things Dave is known for—and it's one of his favorite lessons. Turn to page 31 as I get ready to start the video and think about this: Culture has made buying things on credit a normal part of life. When did you get your first credit card—and why?

Start the Video

As the Video Plays

- [ ] **Update your class's Financial Snapshot.**
Add up the information from the Financial Snapshot cards and enter it into your Coordinator Dashboard. You'll share this information with your class when the video ends.

- [ ] **Update your attendance and watch the video.**
Update your attendance on financialpeace.com or pass around the attendance sheet. Then, follow along with your members in your Coordinator Guide.

LESSON 02

"YOUR *income* IS YOUR MOST **POWERFUL** wealth-building **TOOL.**"

—DAVE RAMSEY

BABY STEP 2

KEY POINTS

Baby Step 2 is paying off all debt (except the house) using the debt snowball.

Debt is not a tool used to build wealth, and payments don't have to be a way of life.

It takes gazelle intensity to get out of debt.

BABY STEP 2

Pay Off All Debt (Except the House) Using the Debt Snowball

You've got $1,000 in the bank and you're ready for Baby Step 2: paying off all your debt except your house using the debt snowball! Attack the smallest debt first while making minimum payments on the others. Once you pay off the first one, you'll move to the next smallest debt, taking your freed-up money, newfound motivation, and momentum with you—until you pay off the last, largest debt!

THE 7 BABY STEPS

LESSON 2 //
BABY STEP 2

GUIDE
Dave Ramsey

BABY STEP 2

Pay off all __DEBT__ (except the house) using the debt snowball.

> "THE RICH RULE OVER THE POOR, AND THE BORROWER IS SLAVE TO THE *lender.*"
>
> PROVERBS 22:7 (NIV)

MYTHS & TRUTHS

MYTH: I need a credit card to rent a car and make purchases online.

TRUTH: You can do both of these things with a __DEBIT__ card.

MYTH: Car payments are a way of life. You can't live without a car payment.

TRUTH: You can stay away from car payments by paying cash for reliable used cars.

ANSWER KEY
Debt
Debit

LESSON 2 //
MYTHS & TRUTHS

MYTH: I need to take out a credit card to build up my credit score.

TRUTH: The FICO score is an "I love ___DEBT___" score.

MYTH: I pay my credit card off every month. And I can earn points and airline miles.

TRUTH: When you use a credit card instead of cash, you actually spend ___MORE___ because you don't feel it.

MYTH: A credit card is more secure than a debit card.

TRUTH: Debit cards and credit cards have the ___SAME___ amount of protection.

MYTH: My teenager needs a credit card to learn how to be responsible with money.

TRUTH: More students drop out of school because of ___FINANCIAL___ trouble than from academic failure.

MYTH: Leasing a car is smart. You should always lease things that go down in value. There are tax advantages.

TRUTH: Consumer Reports and a good calculator will tell you that a car ___LEASE___ is the most expensive way to operate and finance a vehicle.

ANSWER KEY

Debt
More
Same
Financial
Lease

MYTH: I can get a good deal on a new car.

TRUTH: A new car loses ___**60%**___ of its value in the first five years.

MYTH: A home equity loan is a good option for consolidation and a great substitute for an emergency fund.

TRUTH: You don't go into debt when you're in the middle of an emergency. You'll make the emergency a ___**CRISIS**___.

MYTH: Debt consolidation is smart. It saves interest and gets you a smaller payment.

TRUTH: Debt consolidation does nothing to change the ___**BEHAVIOR**___ that got you into debt. So, many actually end up with more debt.

MYTH: Cosigning a loan is okay if I'm helping a friend or relative.

TRUTH: The bank requires a cosigner because the person isn't likely to ___**REPAY**___.

MYTH: You can't go to college without taking out student loans.

TRUTH: ___**68%**___ of millionaires with a college degree never took out student loans.

ANSWER KEY

60%
Crisis
Behavior
Repay
68%

BIGGEST MYTH OF ALL

MYTH: Debt is a tool and should be used to create prosperity.

TRUTH: Debt is proof that the borrower is __SLAVE__ to the lender.

> GIVE NO SLEEP TO YOUR EYES, NOR *slumber* TO YOUR EYELIDS. DELIVER YOURSELF *like a gazelle* FROM THE HAND OF THE HUNTER, AND LIKE A BIRD FROM THE HAND OF THE FOWLER.
>
> PROVERBS 6:4-5 (NKJV)

Notes

ANSWER KEY

Slave

HOW TO GET OUT OF DEBT

- Quit borrowing more ___MONEY___!
- You must ___SAVE___ money.
- ___SELL___ something.
- Take a part-time ___JOB___.
- ___PRAYER___ really works.

DEBT SNOWBALL

List your debts smallest to largest. Make minimum payments on all of them and attack the smallest one with a vengeance.

Pssst...

When the One-Minute Takeaway appears on the video, that's your cue to move toward the front of the room and kick off this lesson's Activity. Turn the page to prepare for what happens next.

one-minute TAKEAWAY

ANSWER KEY

Money
Save
Sell
Job
Prayer

ACTIVITY

When the Video Ends

☐ **After the One-Minute Takeaway, say:**

> As you can tell, getting out of debt is a really big deal! And no matter how much debt you have, you can become debt-free! While we were watching the video, I added up the information from all of our Financial Snapshot cards. Let's take a look at where we stand as a class. And then, we're going to have our very first plasectomy party!

Activity: Financial Snapshot (2 minutes)

☐ **Share your class's Financial Snapshot figures.**
Note: It is not unusual for the total debt to be surprisingly high, even in smaller classes. Members may feel overwhelmed with the state of their finances. Be overly encouraging and reassuring. Then say:

> The biggest takeaway from this information should be that you're not alone. Millions of people who started exactly where you are right now are winning with money!
>
> This information gives you a great picture of where you're starting from, and we can also see where we stand as a class. We'll do this Activity again at the beginning of Lesson 9 so we can see how far we've come.

Activity: It's Time for a Plasectomy (10 minutes)

Get excited for this Activity—even if someone chooses not to cut up their credit cards right now. For those who are cutting them up, applaud and celebrate every single card that is destroyed. This a big step and a major accomplishment toward becoming debt-free.

- ☐ **Direct attention to the Activity on page 36 by saying:**

  > You watched Dave cut up some credit cards on stage. Now it's time for *us* to draw a line in the sand and see if we're up for the challenge. Turn to page 36. Read and complete the Activity to see if it's time for *your* plasectomy!

- ☐ **Pick up your scissors and say:**

  > I'll have scissors with me every lesson, so any time you're ready to cut up your cards, the whole class will encourage you and celebrate with you. Who wants to go first?
  >
  > If you're not feeling ready, would you be willing to share with the class what's holding you back?

- ☐ **Pass the scissors around.**
  After everyone who wants to has cut up their credit cards, say:

  > Congratulations to everyone who took this BIG step toward becoming debt-free. You're choosing to live differently, and it's going to change your life. I'm so proud of you!

When the Activity Ends

- ☐ **Turn to page 76 of this guide for instructions on how to lead your class through the discussion questions.**

LESSON 2 //
ACTIVITY

IT'S TIME FOR A PLASECTOMY

Remember, your situation will never change until you do! So, grab the scissors and slash your lifeline to stupid. You're done with debt, and you're never going back, which means you're done with credit cards. That's right. It's time for a plasectomy.

We get it, this step is hard. But debt has taken too much from you already. And it's the biggest thief of your financial future. So get the cards out of your life and start attacking debt with a vengeance! Goodbye, credit cards. Hello, freedom.

Whether you cut them up in your class or at home on your own, **write down the card information first**! Once you pay them off, you'll have to call and cancel the account.

	CREDIT CARD NAME	PLASECTOMY DATE	CANCEL DATE
1			
2			
3			
4			
5			
6			
7			

HOW TO CLOSE OUT YOUR CREDIT CARDS

The plasectomy is a mental and physical sign that you're done with debt—forever. *No more. No way. No how.* But there are **three steps** to breaking up with your credit cards for good!

1 PAY OFF THE BALANCE

Go ahead and cut up the cards. But before you can cancel the accounts, you'll need to pay off the balance. No matter how much you have to pay off, just list the payments in your debt snowball and attack them with gazelle intensity when it's time to pay them off!

2 CALL THE CREDIT CARD COMPANY

Once you pay off the balance, call the credit card company and say, "I'm calling to close my account." Spoiler alert: They're going to say whatever they can think of to keep you from leaving. Don't fall for their gimmicks or counter offers. Just repeat, "I'm calling to close my account." Be firm and remember, you're *done* with debt.

3 GET IT IN WRITING

When you call to cancel your account, keep a record of the conversation details. You'll want written proof from the company that your account is clear and closed. It's also a good idea to check your credit report later in the year to verify that these accounts are actually closed.

DISCUSSION

Discussion (10 minutes)

- ☐ **Review the discussion questions.**
  Ask for a volunteer to read the first discussion question on page 38 in the Member Workbook.

- ☐ **Get them engaged!**
  Give members a chance to share their responses. Then continue through the list of questions, letting a different member read each question.

Create Interaction and Don't Fear Silence!

Get the discussion started and then let the members take over. There might be silence after you ask a question—that's okay! Give it a few moments. Silence is a powerful motivator. If you need to initiate the discussion, try answering the question and then calling on members by name.

DISCUSSION

Whether you're in a class or online, be honest with your answers and remember to encourage one another!

1. Look over the list of myths and truths Dave covered in the video. Which myths have fooled you in the past? How can you make sure you don't get duped again?

2. What fears or concerns do you have about living without credit cards?

3. Proverbs 22:7 says, " . . . the borrower is slave to the lender" (NIV). What would your life look like if you were totally debt-free? What could you do that you can't afford to do now?

4. Dave says, "You can wander into debt, but you can't wander out." You'll have to make some tough decisions and sacrifices moving forward. What's one area you can cut back—or cut out—to reach your money goals?

5. You need serious passion and motivation to get out of debt. What's one thing you can do to kick-start and keep up your gazelle intensity?

KEEP THE CONVERSATION GOING!

Answer these questions online in the Financial Peace community!

financialpeace.com

ENDING THE LESSON

Wrap-Up (5 minutes)

- ☐ **Direct members to page 39 and read through the Action Steps.** Then say:

  > As a reminder, you need to complete these Action Steps before we meet for the next lesson.

- ☐ **Show members the Baby Step 2 Goal on page 42.** Coordinator, turn to page 82 in this guide! Then say:

  > If you turn to page 42 in your workbooks, you'll see the Baby Step 2 Goal page. The day you pay off your last, biggest debt, come back to this page. Write down the date and celebrate being debt-free!

- ☐ **Encourage members to revisit their budgets by saying:**

  > Be sure you're checking your EveryDollar budget throughout the week to assign transactions and make adjustments. Remember, it will take a few months to get the budget right, so don't get discouraged. I'll be checking in with you each week to see how it's going.

- ☐ **Return the chairs and clean up the space.**

Dismissed!

AFTER THE LESSON

- ☐ **Complete the items on the After Each Lesson checklist on pages 36–37 of this guide.**

ACTION STEPS

It's time to live out what you just learned! Complete each of the Action Steps before the next lesson.

- ☐ **CUT UP YOUR CREDIT CARDS**
  If you didn't do it as part of the Activity, gather the family, grab some scissors, and host a plasectomy party! This should be a celebration because it's the moment you decided to stop the crazy cycle of debt. Just remember that cutting up the cards isn't enough. You also need to call each credit card company and close those life-sucking accounts once and for all.

- ☐ **COMPLETE THE DEBT SNOWBALL**
  Enter your non-mortgage debts in the Debt Snowball Tool on **financialpeace.com.** The tool will automatically sort your debts from smallest to largest so you can start attacking the smallest debt first. Then set a target date for paying off your last, largest debt! Don't have any debt? Great. You're crushing it. Head to Baby Step 3!

- ☐ **SELL EVERYTHING IN SIGHT**
  That old VCR? *It's out.* The bicycle you haven't ridden in years? *Gone.* Old books, old clothes, old furniture? *Sell. It. All.* Have a garage sale, post everything online—get whatever money you can to knock out your current Baby Step!

- ☐ **READ *THE DEBT SNOWBALL* ON THE NEXT PAGE**
  Need a reminder on how the debt snowball really works? We've got you covered! Check out how this method is the fastest way to get rid of every last debt payment.

THE DEBT *Snowball*

What could you do if you didn't owe anyone your paycheck? That means no student loans, no credit card bills, no car payments—no debt. With the **debt snowball**, you'll pay off the smallest debt first and work your way up to the largest. *But wait.* Doesn't it make sense mathematically to pay off the debt with the highest interest rate first? Maybe. But if you'd been paying attention to math, you wouldn't be in debt. It's time to pay attention to your behavior. Enter the debt snowball.

Attack!

1 LIST YOUR DEBTS FROM SMALLEST TO LARGEST.

Don't worry about the interest rates! Seriously—smallest to largest.

2 ATTACK SMALLEST DEBT WITH A VENGEANCE!

Make minimum payments on all your other debts while you pay off the smallest debt as fast as you can!

3 REPEAT THIS METHOD AS YOU PLOW YOUR WAY THROUGH DEBT.

Once that debt is gone, take its payment and apply it to the next smallest debt. The more you pay off, the more your freed-up money grows and gets thrown on the next debt—like a snowball rolling downhill.

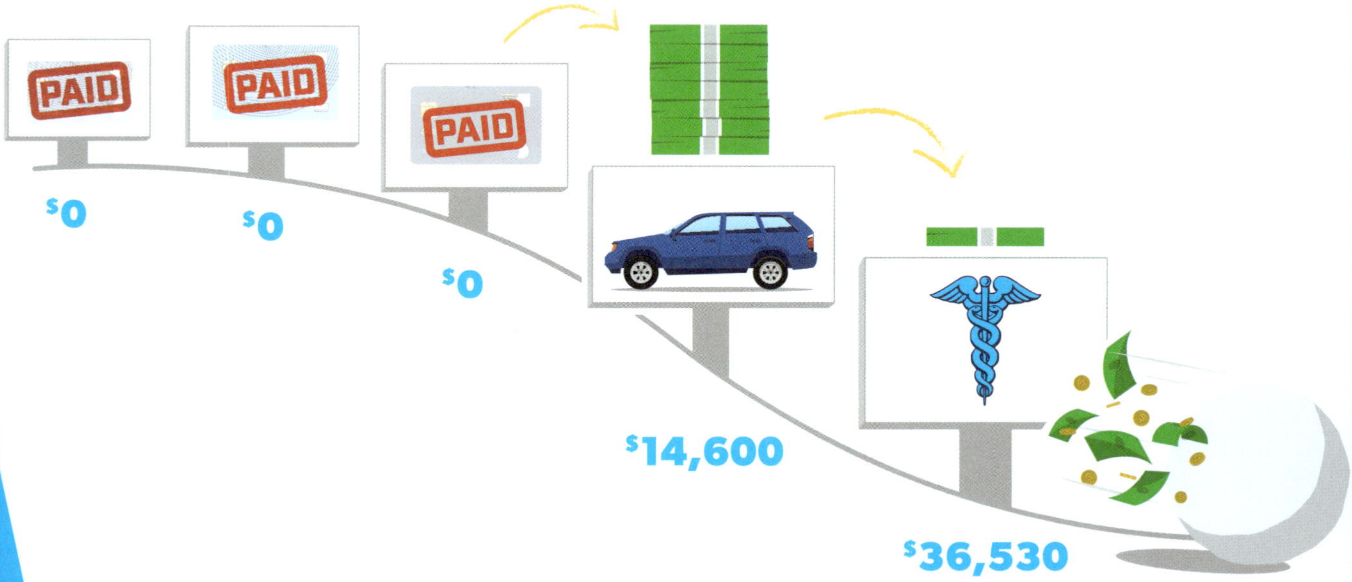

TRACK YOUR PROGRESS ON FINANCIALPEACE.COM.

Use our Debt Snowball Tool to keep up with your attack plan for debt!

BABY STEP 2

Take the total number from your debt snowball and write it below. Then, once you pay off that very last debt, celebrate and come back to this page to mark the day you became debt-free.

GOAL

$

DATE COMPLETED

____ / ____ / ____

MONTH DAY YEAR

You can
WANDER INTO DEBT
but you
CAN'T WANDER OUT.

LESSON 03

BABY STEP 3

LESSON PREP

- While you may see fewer people in your class this week, don't get discouraged! The truth about debt is polarizing and can take members a little while to accept. Encourage them to stick with the course. It *will* be worth it!
- This lesson will show members the step in the plan when they can stop paying someone else and start paying themselves. If they are still on Baby Step 1 or 2, members might be tempted to jump ahead. But remind them that it's important to do the Baby Steps in order.
- From this point on, plan to bring scissors to every lesson and encourage members to cut up their credit cards whenever they're ready.

START THE LESSON

Welcome and Review (5 minutes)

☐ **Welcome class members back.**
Show how excited you are about this lesson.

☐ **Celebrate plasectomies!**
Call for a show of hands of class members who cut up any credit cards since the last lesson. Celebrate each of those members. Remind your class that you have scissors for anyone who is ready to cut up their credit cards today!

- ☐ **Have a budget checkup! Say:**

  > How are you adjusting to living on a budget?
  >
  > What are some categories that you forgot to include when you made your budget originally? How did you adjust for those categories?

- ☐ **Review the Action Steps from the previous lesson.**
  Check to make sure class members completed the Action Steps from Lesson 2. Address any questions or concerns from class members, then say:

  > Who sold some stuff to put money toward the Baby Step you're on?

Get Ready for the Video

- ☐ **Introduce the video by saying:**

  > In this lesson, you'll learn about Baby Step 3, your fully funded emergency fund. Turn to page 47 as I get ready to start the video and think about this: If something came up that required you to be away from work for three or four months without pay, what would you do?

Start the Video

As the Video Plays

- ☐ **Update your attendance and watch the video.**
  Update your attendance on financialpeace.com or pass around the attendance sheet. Then, follow along with your members in your Coordinator Guide.

LESSON 03

"HAVING AN **EMERGENCY FUND** is like a breath of *fresh air.*"

—RACHEL CRUZE

BABY STEP 3

KEY POINTS

Baby Step 3 is saving 3–6 months of expenses in a fully funded emergency fund.

The emergency fund is Murphy repellent. It keeps you from living in fear of the next emergency.

Your emergency fund is insurance, not an investment! It prevents you from going back into debt.

BABY STEP

3

Save 3–6 Months of Expenses in a Fully Funded Emergency Fund

Baby Step 3 is all about building your full emergency fund with 3–6 months of expenses. After the momentum and intensity of Baby Step 2, it's easy to let your foot off the gas. Don't let that happen! Keep your intensity through Baby Step 3. In the same way your $1,000 starter emergency fund kept you from going into debt because of emergency expenses, your fully funded emergency fund will protect you when life's bigger surprises hit.

THE 7 BABY STEPS

GUIDE
Rachel Cruze

SAVING

> “DEBT STEALS YOUR FUTURE.
> *Saving secures it.*
> WITH DEBT, YOU OWE. WITH SAVING, YOU OWN.”
>
> —RACHEL CRUZE

Nearly 80% of Americans live paycheck to paycheck. They use ___DEBT___ to cover emergencies.

The emergency fund gives you ___CASH___ to cover emergencies so you stay out of debt.

You can save money if it’s your ___PRIORITY___.

> “THE WISE MAN *saves* FOR THE FUTURE, BUT THE FOOLISH MAN *spends* WHATEVER HE GETS.”
>
> PROVERBS 21:20 (TLB)

ANSWER KEY

Debt
Cash
Priority

The ___CURE___ for comparisons is contentment.

___GRATITUDE___ will lead you to contentment.

> "I AM NOT SAYING THIS BECAUSE I AM IN NEED, FOR I HAVE **LEARNED TO BE** *content* WHATEVER THE CIRCUMSTANCES."
>
> PHILIPPIANS 4:11 (NIV)

BABY STEP 3

GUIDE
Chris Hogan

Save ___3–6___ ___MONTHS___ of expenses in a fully funded emergency fund.

Murphy's Law states: Anything that can go wrong ___WILL___ go wrong.

Notes

ANSWER KEY

Cure
Gratitude
3–6 Months
Will

LESSON 3 //
BABY STEP 3

If your income is unstable, you should rely more on a six-month emergency fund. If you have a stable income, you can lean more toward a three-month emergency fund.

An emergency fund is ___INSURANCE___. It's not an investment.

When you use it, ___BUILD___ it back up.

> **AN INTELLIGENT *heart* ACQUIRES KNOWLEDGE,**
> **AND THE EAR OF THE WISE SEEKS KNOWLEDGE.**
>
> PROVERBS 18:15 (ESV)

Pssst...

When the One-Minute Takeaway appears on the video, that's your cue to move toward the front of the room and kick off this lesson's Activity. Turn the page to prepare for what happens next.

one-minute **TAKEAWAY**

____

____

____

____

ANSWER KEY

Insurance
Build

ACTIVITY

When the Video Ends

- ☐ **After the One-Minute Takeaway, say:**

  So you heard about contentment from Rachel, and you learned about the importance of having an emergency fund from Chris. This will protect you against Murphy and from going back into debt. That's why it's so important to stay gazelle intense through Baby Step 3. Let's do a case study that shows us how to do that.

Activity: Stay Gazelle Intense (8 minutes)

- ☐ **Introduce the case study on page 50 by saying:**

  Turn to page 50 and let's look at the case study about two couples who are saving for Baby Step 3. Work through the case study. Then we'll discuss the answers, as well as how you can stay focused even after you're debt-free.

- ☐ **After a few minutes, ask for the results of the case study.**
  See below for answers:

  Answer: Because both couples have already saved $1,000 from Baby Step 1, they need $11,000 to finish their emergency fund.

  It will take Will and Claire nearly 37 months. The math for that is $11,000 divided by $300.

  Because Joe and Kate were gazelle intense, it will take them just 11 months. The math for that is $11,000 divided by $1,000.

- ☐ **Discuss the two follow-up questions as a class.**

Activity: It's Time for a Plasectomy (5 minutes)

- ☐ **Introduce another opportunity for a plasectomy by saying:**

  Getting out of debt is a BIG deal! You should absolutely celebrate that when the time comes, but as we saw in the Activity, you do not want to let off the gas! The faster you can get through the first three Baby Steps, the sooner you get to build wealth and give.

  Baby Step 3 is all about using cash instead of credit cards to cover emergencies. You don't want to go back into debt! So, who's ready to cut up their credit cards?

- ☐ **Pass the scissors around.**
  After everyone who wants to has cut up their credit cards, celebrate them!

When the Activity Ends

- ☐ **Turn to page 96 of this guide for instructions on how to lead your class through the discussion questions.**

STAY GAZELLE *Intense!*

Let's look at two couples. We'll call them **Will & Claire** and **Joe & Kate**.

Both couples were gazelle intense and made extreme sacrifices to pay off their debt. They're finally debt-free! Baby Step 2—check! They take a few weeks to breathe and celebrate before they dive into Baby Step 3.

But now, they're ready to get their **fully funded emergency fund** up and running! They look at their current savings and expenses and decide on their emergency fund goal.

HERE ARE THEIR *Numbers*

$1,000	CURRENT EMERGENCY FUND
$2,000	CURRENT MONTHLY EXPENSES
$12,000	FULLY FUNDED EMERGENCY FUND GOAL

Both couples are single-income households and need a 6-month emergency fund!

HOW TO SAVE FOR BABY STEP 3

With $1,000 already in the bank from Baby Step 1, how many months will it take each couple to reach their $12,000 goal?

WILL & CLAIRE

Will and Claire continue celebrating and let off the gas. They only put **$300 per month** into their emergency fund.

37

MONTHS

JOE & KATE

Joe and Kate stay gazelle intense and put the **$1,000 per month** that *was* going toward debt right into their emergency fund.

11

MONTHS

Moral of the story? **Don't let off the gas!** Take what you were throwing at debt and save it in your fully funded emergency fund. Keep up your gazelle intensity through Baby Step 3!

Respond to the following questions:

1. Remember to stay gazelle intense in Baby Step 3. But what's the one way you'll celebrate being debt-free before you kick it back into high gear?

2. If these couples asked you about investing or paying off their mortgage before completing Baby Step 3, what advice would you give them? Why?

DISCUSSION

Discussion (10 minutes)

- ☐ **Review the discussion questions.**
  Ask for a volunteer to read the first discussion question on page 52.

- ☐ **Get them engaged!**
  Give members a chance to share their responses. Then continue through the list of questions, letting a different member read each question.

Create Interaction and Don't Fear Silence!

Get the discussion started and then let the members take over. There might be silence after you ask a question—that's okay! Give it a few moments. Silence is a powerful motivator. If you need to initiate the discussion, try answering the question and then calling on members by name.

DISCUSSION

Whether you're in a class or online, be honest with your answers and remember to encourage one another!

1. By now, you've seen and experienced the power of the debt snowball. How can its momentum help you knock out your emergency fund? Why is that important to know?

2. When have you wished you had Murphy repellent in your life? How would a full emergency fund have turned that crisis into a simple inconvenience?

3. In building your emergency fund, consider the suggested savings range of 3–6 months of expenses. Which amount makes the most sense for your life and gives you the most peace?

4. Once you're debt-free, it can be tempting to let your foot off the gas and taper off the intensity. But we want you to move through the first three Baby Steps as fast as you can! What are some practical things you can do to maintain your gazelle intensity in Baby Step 3?

KEEP THE CONVERSATION GOING!

Answer these questions online in the Financial Peace community!

financialpeace.com

ENDING THE LESSON

Wrap-Up (5 minutes)

- ☐ **Direct members to page 53 and read through the Action Steps. Then say:**

  As a reminder, you need to complete these Action Steps before we meet for the next lesson.

- ☐ **Show members the Baby Step 3 Goal on page 56.** Coordinator, turn to page 102 in this guide. Then say:

  Turn to page 56. When you're ready for Baby Step 3, figure out what amount your fully funded emergency fund needs to be. Come to this page and write that number down. When you reach your goal, come back to this page and mark the date you finished Baby Step 3!

- ☐ **Remind members to keep working their budget. Say:**

  Budgeting isn't a one-and-done thing. Make sure you're getting into the habit of assigning transactions in EveryDollar and adjusting any categories throughout the week to stay on track!

- ☐ **Return the chairs and clean up the space.**

Dismissed!

AFTER THE LESSON

- ☐ **Complete the items on the After Each Lesson checklist on pages 36–37 of this guide.**

LESSON 3 //
BABY STEP 3

ACTION STEPS

It's time to live out what you just learned! Complete each of the Action Steps before the next lesson.

☐ **CALCULATE HOW MUCH YOU NEED FOR YOUR FULLY FUNDED EMERGENCY FUND**

It's time to outwit Murphy! The first step to saving 3–6 months of expenses is figuring out how much you really need. You'll have to answer two questions: How stable or unstable is your income? That helps you determine whether you need closer to three or six months of expenses saved. What are the main expenses in your budget? Crunch some numbers, and you've got a Baby Step 3 goal.

☐ **ROLL THAT SNOWBALL TOWARD BABY STEP 3**

When you reach Baby Step 3, you will have spent months—maybe even years—rolling your debt snowball with gazelle intensity. But now, every cent goes to you, not Sallie Mae or credit card companies. When you're ready for Baby Step 3, create an emergency fund category and just redirect those hard-working snowball dollars right into that fund.

☐ **READ *WHERE TO SAVE BABY STEP 3* ON THE NEXT PAGE**

A money market account is a smart Baby Step 3 choice. Why? These accounts keep your cash safe and accessible. Read on to learn about the account options available to you.

WHERE TO SAVE BABY STEP 3

You're going to throw all your debt snowball dollars into savings, you've convinced yourself rice and beans aren't *all* that bad, and you promise to keep the second job you're dying to quit—all for Baby Step 3. This is *insurance* after all. This is what will keep you from going back into debt. This is your protection from life's emergencies!

So, how do you keep it safe?

Three words: **money market account.**

Because you need to protect your hard-earned cash (security) and still get to it when you need it (liquidity), you'll keep your emergency fund in a money market account.

Money market accounts offer security, liquidity, and a *little* bit of interest. It won't earn you much, but we aren't concerned with making money here! Remember, Baby Step 3 is *insurance*, not an investment.

Insurance—**NOT AN INVESTMENT**

THREE OPTIONS WHEN OPENING A MONEY MARKET ACCOUNT:

1. **LOCAL BANK** MONEY MARKET ACCOUNT
Most of these accounts offer higher interest rates for larger balances, along with debit cards or check-writing privileges. Some even let you move money electronically. Finally, bank deposits are insured by the Federal Deposit Insurance Corporation (FDIC) for up to $250,000.

2. **ONLINE BANK** MONEY MARKET ACCOUNT
In general, these types of accounts offer better interest rates and still offer the liquidity and security of a local bank. But like everything else with your money, you need to do plenty of research first. Check out what's available and get what works best for you.

3. **MUTUAL FUND** MONEY MARKET INVESTMENT ACCOUNT
These accounts might give you a higher return—but there's more risk. Rates can fluctuate, and you may lose money in the short term. While they aren't insured by the FDIC, they are designed to be secure—though you may have more restrictions on using the money.

> **Don't let the options confuse you.** The important thing is to get your money in a secure, accessible account. You're saving up for an inevitable emergency, which means doing nothing is *not* an option. So, do your research, open an account, and keep up your intensity!

BABY STEP 3

Write your Baby Step 3 goal below and bookmark this page. On the day you save your last dollar in Baby Step 3, you'll see how all your hard work paid off!

GOAL

$

DATE COMPLETED

_____ / _____ / _____
MONTH DAY YEAR

An Emergency FUND TURNS A CRISIS INTO *an inconvenience.*

LESSON 04

BABY STEPS 4 5 6 7

LESSON PREP

- Most class members will still have some questions related to budgeting and how to work the debt snowball. If you're comfortable, answer any questions you can or direct them to the Ask a Coach feature on financialpeace.com.
- This lesson covers Baby Steps 4–7. That's a lot of information shared in a short amount of time, so members may have more questions than usual. Most of their questions will be answered in the next five lessons, so encourage them to keep attending every single lesson.
- While most of your class will be on Baby Steps 1 and 2, emphasize the importance of this lesson. It will help them start dreaming for their future and show them that no matter where they are in the Baby Steps, there is a clear path to financial peace.

START THE LESSON

Welcome and Review (5 minutes)

☐ **Welcome class members back.**
Take a couple of minutes to address any questions class members may have at this point, specifically related to Baby Steps 1–3. Remember, "I don't know" is a totally acceptable answer! Say this:

> We've covered a lot of information in the last few lessons. What questions do you have about Baby Steps 1, 2, or 3?

- [ ] **Have a budget checkup! Say:**

  “ It’s time for our budget checkup. What categories do you need to adjust or add?

  Which category has been or will be a budget buster? What can you do to make that less of a danger?

  > Note: If members need help answering the last question, remind them that cashing out categories can help them avoid overspending.

- [ ] **Review the Action Steps from the previous lesson.**
  Check to make sure that members determined what a Baby Step 3 emergency fund would look like for them (don’t ask for their specific amounts).

Get Ready for the Video

- [ ] **Introduce the video by saying:**

  “ In this lesson, you’re going to hear about Baby Steps 4–7. Don’t let that overwhelm you. Most of you are probably on Baby Step 1 or Baby Step 2. This lesson gives you a quick look at the rest of the Baby Steps.

  As I get ready to start the video, turn to page 61 in your workbook and consider this: What do you want your life to look like twenty years, or even forty years, from now? How are you going to get there?

Start the Video

As the Video Plays

Update your attendance on financialpeace.com or pass around the attendance sheet. Then, follow along with your members in your Coordinator Guide.

LESSON 04

“INVESTING NOW WILL *replace* YOUR PAYCHECK LATER.”

—CHRIS HOGAN

BABY STEPS 4 5 6 7

KEY POINTS

Baby Step 4 is to invest 15% of your household income in retirement.

Baby Step 5 is to save for your children's college fund.

Baby Step 6 is to pay off your home early.

Baby Step 7 is to build wealth and give.

You'll do Baby Steps 4–6 in order, but at the same time. Then, Baby Step 7 is where you'll have the most fun!

BABY STEP

4

Invest 15% of Your Household Income in Retirement

You've finished paying for the past; now it's time to start paying for your future! On Baby Step 4, you'll invest 15% of your household income into tax-favored accounts for retirement. There is no quick-fix, snap-your-fingers way to build wealth, but you *can* become an everyday millionaire. The key is to start investing early, consistently, and let compound interest work its magic!

THE 7 BABY STEPS

GUIDE
Chris Hogan

chrishogan360.com

BABY STEP 4

Invest __15%__ of your household income in retirement.

Investing __$150__ every month from age 25 to 65 (at 11% rate of return) gets you to $1.3 million.

Have a __DREAM__ __MEETING__ with your spouse. If you're single, talk with your accountability partner.

> **"IT DOESN'T MATTER WHERE YOU'VE BEEN. IT MATTERS** *where you're going.*"
>
> —CONDOLEEZZA RICE

Numbers change when __PEOPLE__ do.

When you invest 15% of your income every month, you can become an __EVERYDAY__ millionaire.

> "*Good planning* **AND HARD WORK LEAD TO PROSPERITY, BUT HASTY SHORTCUTS LEAD TO POVERTY.**"
>
> PROVERBS 21:5 (NLT)

ANSWER KEY

15%
$150
Dream Meeting
People
Everyday

The Story of JACK & BLAKE

AND THE POWER OF COMPOUND INTEREST

JACK

Jack started investing at the age of 21. He invested $2,400 every year for nine years and then he stopped.

At age 30, Jack put in zero dollars—**zero**! That means *he* stopped but his money *didn't*.

BLAKE

Blake didn't start investing until age 30. He invested $2,400 every year until the age of 67—that's **38 years**!

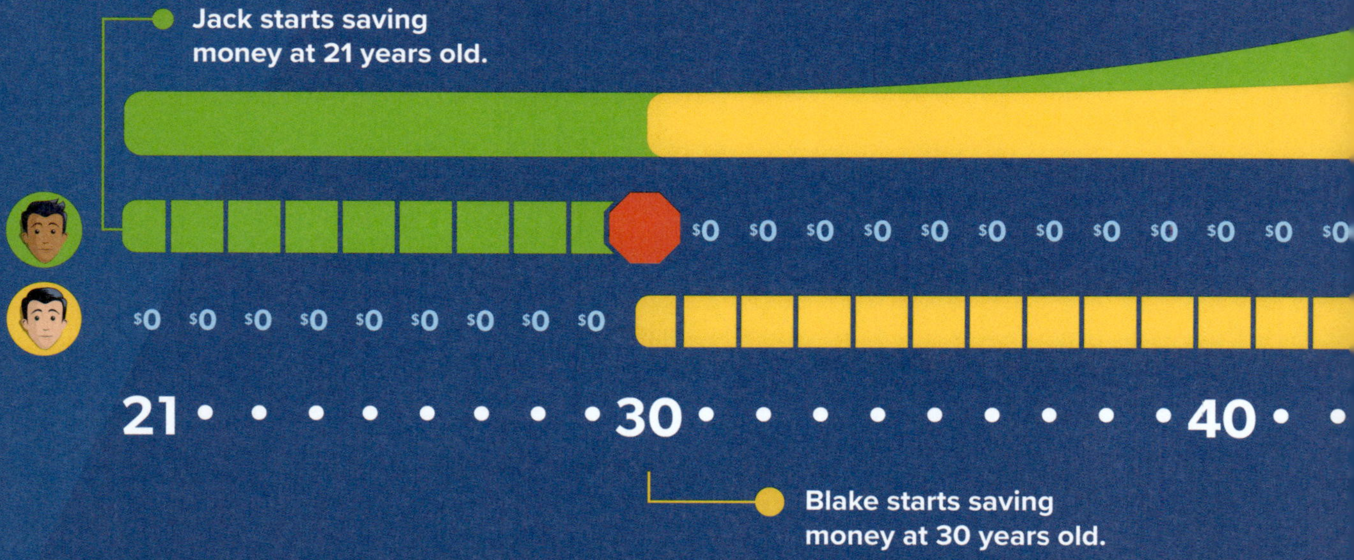

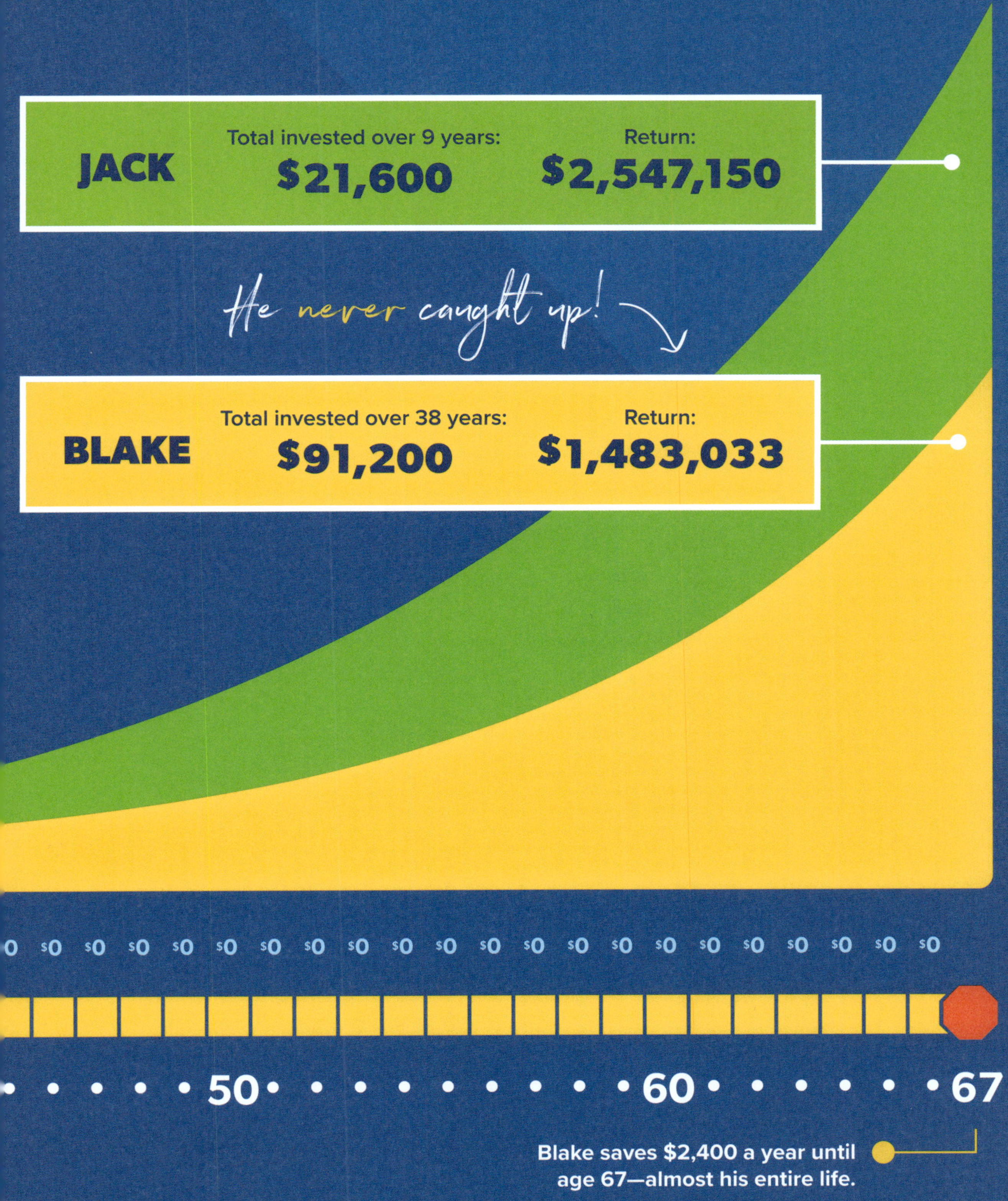

THE MORAL OF THE STORY IS START EARLY!

BABY STEP

5

Save for Your Children's College Fund

By this step, you've paid off all your debt except the house and you've started saving for retirement. Now it's time to save for your children's college expenses using an Education Savings Account (ESA) or a 529 plan. Help your children go to college the right way—without debt. It *can* be done!

THE 7 BABY STEPS

GUIDE
Rachel Cruze

BABY STEP 5

Save for your children's __COLLEGE__ fund.

$2000/yr. tax free

You have two options for college savings—an __ESA__ and a __529__ plan.

> “TRAIN UP A *child* IN THE WAY HE SHOULD GO, AND WHEN HE IS OLD HE WILL NOT *depart* FROM IT.”
>
> PROVERBS 22:6 (NKJV)

Three ways to go to college debt-free:

1. Select an __AFFORDABLE__ school.
2. __APPLY__ for things like scholarships, grants, and work study.
3. Get a __JOB__.

> “COLLEGE IS A BLESSING, NOT AN *entitlement.*”
>
> —RACHEL CRUZE

ANSWER KEY

College
ESA
529
Affordable
Apply
Job

BABY STEP

6

Pay Off Your Home Early

Baby Step 6 is the big one! There's only one more thing standing in the way of your complete freedom from debt—your mortgage. This part of paying off debt is a little more like a marathon. But any extra money you can put toward your mortgage will help save you tens of thousands of dollars in interest. And the grass will truly feel different under your feet once it's *yours*.

THE 7 BABY STEPS

GUIDE
Dave Ramsey

BABY STEP 6

Pay off your home __EARLY__.

100% of foreclosures occur on a home with a __MORTGAGE__.

Should you PAY OFF YOUR HOME?

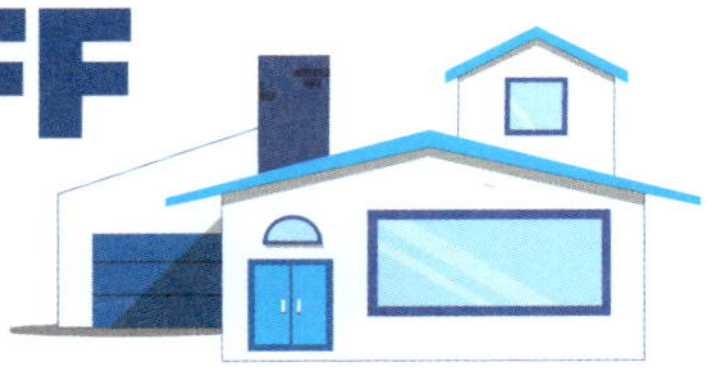

INTEREST vs. TAXES

The interest you pay on your mortgage is deductible on your taxes. Are you saving more money by taking this deduction or should you just pay the taxes? Let's take a look.

MORTGAGE INTEREST

$200K	x	5%	=	$10,000
MORTGAGE AMOUNT		INTEREST RATE		ANNUAL INTEREST PAID

TAXES WITH PAID HOME

$10K	x	22%	=	$2,200
TAXABLE AMOUNT		TAX BRACKET		TAXES PAID

SO, WHAT MAKES MORE SENSE . . .

PAYING $10,000 TO A BANK OR PAYING $2,200 TO THE IRS?

ANSWER KEY

Early
Mortgage

BABY STEP 7

Build Wealth and Give

You know what people with no debt and no payments can do? Anything they want! Now you can truly live and give like no one else by building wealth, becoming insanely generous, and changing your family tree. Your focus and sacrifice got you here. You made it. You lived like no one else, and now you get to *live* and *give* like no one else!

THE 7 BABY STEPS

GUIDE
Dave Ramsey

BABY STEP 7

Build wealth and be outrageously ___GENEROUS___!

Giving is possibly the most ___FUN___ you will ever have with money.

> "EACH OF YOU SHOULD **GIVE WHAT YOU HAVE DECIDED IN YOUR HEART TO** *give,* NOT RELUCTANTLY OR UNDER COMPULSION, FOR GOD **LOVES A CHEERFUL GIVER.**"
>
> 2 CORINTHIANS 9:7 (NIV)

Pssst...

When the One-Minute Takeaway appears on the video, that's your cue to move toward the front of the room and kick off this lesson's Activity. Turn the page to prepare for what happens next.

one-minute TAKEAWAY

____

____

____

____

____

____

ANSWER KEY

Generous
Fun

ACTIVITY

When the Video Ends

☐ **After the One-Minute Takeaway, say:**

I know that was a lot of information to take in, but don't worry. We'll dive deeper into most of those topics in the next five lessons, so make sure you don't miss any of them. For now, let's do a quick review of Baby Steps 4–7.

What is Baby Step 4?

What is Baby Step 5?

What is Baby Step 6?

And lastly, what is Baby Step 7?

☐ **Wait for the class to respond, then say:**

Depending on which Baby Step you're on right now, even thinking about Baby Steps 4–7 may seem like a long way off. But it's important to see how this whole plan works together and start dreaming about what your future could look like. This Activity will help you get specific about what those dreams could be.

Activity: Dream for Your Future (10 minutes)

☐ **Introduce the Activity on page 70 by saying:**

> Let's turn to page 70 and we'll take a few minutes to work through the Activity.

☐ **Allow time for members to complete the Activity.**
Before you ask the first question, take a few minutes to kick off the Activity discussion by sharing *your* dream retirement. Then ask:

> Does anyone want to share their dream retirement?
>
> How will some of you have fun spending your money?
>
> How will some of you have fun giving your money?

☐ **Allow different people to give answers and be encouraging.**
Dreaming about the future should be exciting, even if members are still a long way off from Baby Step 4. Encourage them to let this Activity be motivating!

When the Activity Ends

☐ **Turn to page 122 of this guide for instructions on how to lead your class through the discussion questions.**

LESSON 4 //
ACTIVITY

Dream FOR YOUR FUTURE

You wake up to silence and sun. There's no alarm clock ringing in your ear. In fact, there's no clock in your bedroom at all. You reach for your phone out of habit and put it back on your nightstand before rolling over in bed. **There's a lot you used to do that you don't have to do anymore.**

You don't check your **inbox**—you couldn't even if you wanted to. You retired years ago, long before your coworkers.

You don't check **social media** when you first wake up. You quit the comparison game back when you learned the power of contentment. Plus, you're living your dream. You don't want someone else's life—you love yours.

You don't check your **bank account**. You know how much you have because you know what you're worth—it's somewhere in the ballpark of seven figures.

You don't check the list of what you must do. You get to list what you want to do. **So, what do you want to do?**

WHAT'S YOUR DREAM RETIREMENT?

Get specific! Want to travel? Write where you want to go. Want to live closer to your kids? Jot down what your dream home looks like. Want to start a business? Put it on paper!

IT'S TIME TO LIVE AND GIVE LIKE NO ONE ELSE.

You're living your dream retirement! You're traveling the way you always wanted. You're spending more time with your kids—and maybe even your grandkids. You own your home—and not just any house on the block, your *dream* home.

You've worked hard for years and years to get to where you are today. And it was *all* worth it.

YOU'RE ON BABY STEP 7!

Now you get to have some serious fun with money.

1. You just heard Dave tell the story of his friend who took his entire family on a cruise. **How will you have fun spending your money?**

2. You also heard Dave tell the story of this same friend taking his entire family to give bikes away to kids in need. **How will you have fun giving your money?**

DISCUSSION

Discussion (8 minutes)

- ☐ **Review the discussion questions.**
  Ask for a volunteer to read the first discussion question on page 72.

- ☐ **Get them engaged!**
  Give members a chance to share their responses. Then continue through the list of questions, letting a different member read each question.

Create Interaction and Don't Fear Silence!

Get the discussion started and then let the members take over. There might be silence after you ask a question—that's okay! Give it a few moments. Silence is a powerful motivator. If you need to initiate the discussion, try answering the question and then calling on members by name.

DISCUSSION

Whether you're in a class or online, be honest with your answers and remember to encourage one another!

1. What has been your plan for retirement up to this point? How has this lesson changed the way you think about saving for and dreaming about retirement?

2. If you're a parent, how do you feel about investing for retirement before saving for your children's college fund? Based on the ages of your kids, what is your plan to send them to college debt-free?

3. If you're currently paying a mortgage each month, how would paying off your home early change your life? What would you be able to do that you can't do now?

4. When is a time that generosity has impacted your life? Were you the giver or the receiver?

KEEP THE CONVERSATION GOING!

Answer these questions online in the Financial Peace community!

financialpeace.com

ENDING THE LESSON

Wrap-Up (3 minutes)

- ☐ **Direct members to page 73 and read through the Action Steps. Then say:**

  Some of the Action Steps in this lesson only apply to people on Baby Steps 4, 5, or 6, but the first two apply to everyone! Let's read through the whole list to see what each of you need to do before the next lesson.

- ☐ **Offer budget form guidance by saying:**

  As you get ready for your next Budget Committee Meeting, take note of all of the changes you've made to your EveryDollar budget over the last few weeks and make sure they make it into your next budget.

  I also want to remind you about the forms in the back of your workbook for those of you with irregular incomes, or for those of you who want to budget by when you get paid. As always, let me know how I can help with any budget questions.

- ☐ **Reset the room.**
  Return the chairs and clean up the space.

Dismissed!

AFTER THE LESSON

- ☐ **Complete the items on the After Each Lesson checklist on pages 36–37 of this guide.**

LESSON 4 //
BABY STEPS 4, 5, 6 & 7

ACTION STEPS

It's time to live out what you just learned! Complete each of the Action Steps before the next lesson.

- [ ] **SCHEDULE A BUDGET COMMITTEE MEETING**
You're coming up on your next budgeting cycle! Remember, it takes about three months to get the budget right, so don't get frustrated. If you're married, schedule your next Budget Committee Meeting. Singles, don't forget to review your budget with your accountability partner.

- [ ] **MAKE SURE GIVING IS AT THE TOP OF YOUR BUDGET**
When you hold money with an open hand—not a clenched fist—you're able to give generously *and* receive graciously. No matter which Baby Step you're on, giving is your priority, whether that's a tithe to your church or contributions to charity.

- [ ] **CONTACT A SMARTVESTOR PRO**
If you're ready for Baby Step 4, check out our list of SmartVestor Pros near you at **financialpeace.com**. These investing professionals will help you invest the right way!

- [ ] **RESEARCH ESAS OR 529 PLANS AND SCHOLARSHIPS**
You can also connect with a SmartVestor Pro to start an Education Savings Account (ESA) or a 529 plan. If your teen is closer to college, help them find scholarships to apply for instead. Remember, debt-free college is the *only* option!

- [ ] **READ *IN ORDER, BUT AT THE SAME TIME* ON THE NEXT PAGE**
The Baby Steps work when you do them in order. But Baby Steps 4–6 are done at the same time! We know that sounds confusing, but this deep dive tells you exactly what we mean.

BABY STEPS 4 5 6

IN ORDER, BUT AT THE SAME TIME

You do Baby Steps 1, 2, and 3 one at a time. Check. You do Baby Steps 4, 5, and 6 at the same time. *What?*

Baby Steps 1, 2, and 3 require laser focus and gazelle intensity—and they each have a specific dollar goal. After Baby Step 3, however, the plan changes gears. You'll do Steps 4, 5, and 6 in order, but at the same time.

Here's what we mean:

Meet the Campbells.

This average American family has a household income of $5,000 per month. They used the debt snowball to send $1,500 per month to pay off all their debt. Then they used the *same* gazelle intensity and saved $1,500 per month to finish their emergency fund.

The Campbells celebrate! They get to ease up on their intensity some, but they're ready to attack **Baby Steps 4, 5, and 6—in order, but at the same time**.

IF THEY SET ASIDE $1,000 FOR THESE BABY STEPS, WATCH WHAT WOULD HAPPEN:

1 START BABY STEP 4

The Campbells save 15% of their gross income in retirement. So, they open a Roth 401(k) and start investing $750 every month.

2 START BABY STEP 5

They open an ESA for their 3-year-old and contribute $166 per month. (That's the ESA contribution limit as of 2018.)

3 START BABY STEP 6

The Campbells still have $84! They go ahead and add it to their mortgage payment knowing they could find more money in the budget to throw at their home if they wanted to.

There you have it. Baby Steps 4, 5, and 6—**IN ORDER, BUT AT THE SAME TIME.**

LESSON 05

BUYER BEWARE

LESSON PREP

- The videos in these next five lessons will look different than the first four. Lesson 5 is also the first of the next few lessons that will help class members understand what living on the plan looks like. (Refer to pages 8–9 for the Course Overview.)
- After hearing all 7 Baby Steps, some members may feel overwhelmed by their debt and the amount of money they need to save. Reassure them that others have been where they are and have *won* with their money!
- Since these lessons aren't tied to specific Baby Steps, some members might be confused about where they fit in the plan. Remind them that some principles (like the next two lessons: *Buyer Beware* and *The Role of Insurance*) are important no matter where they are in the Baby Steps.

START THE LESSON

Welcome and Review (5 minutes)

☐ **Welcome class members back by saying:**

> Welcome to Lesson 5! We're halfway through the course! The next five lessons are all about life on the plan. Everything we learn next is to help you move forward in the Baby Steps and make sure you don't lose your momentum or throw off any progress you've made.

☐ **Review the Baby Steps and the Course Overview.**
This is a good time to review the 7 Baby Steps. Encourage class members to try and share them from memory. They are found on pages 6–9 of your Coordinator Guide, and pages 4–7 of the Member Workbook.

☐ **Have a budget checkup!**
At this point, class members will be in their second month of budgeting. Discuss the following questions:

> How has budgeting impacted the way you save and spend?
>
> If you're married, how has budgeting with your spouse helped you talk about money?

☐ **Review the Action Steps from the previous lesson.**
Check to make sure class members completed the Action Steps from Lesson 4. Address any questions or concerns they may have.

Get Ready for the Video

☐ **Introduce the video by saying:**

> As I get ready to start the video, turn to page 78 in your workbook and think about this: In the past month, how often have impulse purchases (things you didn't plan on buying) impacted your budget?

Start the Video

As the Video Plays

Update your attendance on financialpeace.com or pass around the attendance sheet. Then, follow along with your members in your Coordinator Guide.

LESSON 05

"In a *heart* **filled with gratitude** there is no room for discontentment."

—Rachel Cruze

BUYER BEWARE

KEY POINTS

There are a million marketing tactics trying to get at your money and bust your budget.

You *can* have power over your purchases.

Contentment keeps your stuff from owning you.

GUIDE
Dave Ramsey

CAVEAT EMPTOR

Companies use every angle to aggressively compete for your __MONEY__.

We live in the __MOST__ marketed-to culture in the history of the world.

MAJOR WAYS COMPANIES MARKET TO US

Same as cash
↓88% don't pay it off in 90 days
89% finance new car

1. __PERSONAL__ selling
2. __FINANCING__ and __CONVENIENT__ payment methods as a marketing tool
3. TV, radio, magazines, __INTERNET__ and other media
4. Product __POSITIONING__
    - Brand recognition
    - Color
    - Shelf position and packaging

SIGNIFICANT PURCHASES

A "significant purchase" is normally anything over __$300__.

Our bodies go through physiological __CHANGES__ when making a significant purchase.

ANSWER KEY

Money
Most
Personal
Financing
Convenient
Internet
Positioning
$300
Changes

LESSON 5 //
BUYER BEWARE

Notes

POWER OVER PURCHASE

- Wait ____OVERNIGHT____ before making a significant purchase.
- Carefully consider your buying ____MOTIVES____.
- Never buy anything that you do not ____UNDERSTAND____.
- Consider the "____OPPORTUNITY____ cost" of your money.
- Seek the ____COUNSEL____ of your spouse.

> "QUIT CHASING HAPPINESS *with stuff.*"
> —DAVE RAMSEY

ANSWER KEY

Overnight
Motives
Understand
Opportunity
Counsel

GUIDE
Rachel Cruze

7 TIPS FOR NEGOTIATING

1. Always tell the absolute ___TRUTH___.
2. Use the power of ___CASH___.
3. Understand and use ___WALK___-___AWAY___ power.
4. Learn to ___SHUT___ ___UP___.
5. Say, "That's not good ___ENOUGH___!"
6. Identify the ___GOOD___ guy, ___BAD___ guy technique.
7. Master the "if I ___TAKE___ away" technique.

Pssst...

When the One-Minute Takeaway appears on the video, that's your cue to move toward the front of the room and kick off this lesson's Activity. See the next page to prepare for what happens next.

one-minute
TAKEAWAY

ANSWER KEY

Truth
Cash
Walk-Away
Shut Up
Enough
Good
Bad
Take

ACTIVITY

When the Video Ends

- ☐ **After the One-Minute Takeaway, say:**

  Most of us know we're the target of marketing, but we don't realize just *how much* we're marketed to. And all these different companies have one thing in mind—getting us to spend our money. That makes living on a budget even more important. Let's begin to apply the principles we learned from this lesson with our Activity.

- ☐ **Turn the page for instructions on leading your class through the Activity.**

ACTIVITY

Activity: Needs & Wants Quiz (8 minutes)

- ☐ **Introduce the Needs & Wants Quiz on page 81 by saying:**

  On page 81 of your workbook, you'll find a fun quiz to help you think about the differences between wants and needs. If you're married, work with your spouse. If you're here alone, partner up with another person. Think through each item as you work through the list together. If you disagree on some items, dig in and figure out why.

- ☐ **After the Activity, discuss the two follow-up questions as a class.**

When the Activity Ends

- ☐ **Turn to page 138 of this guide for instructions on how to lead your class through the discussion questions.**

LESSON 5 //
ACTIVITY

WHAT TO DO:

If you've ever messed up the budget, you probably overspent on wants by convincing yourself they were needs. In the quiz, mark each item as a want or a need. If you're married, discuss the items where you and your spouse disagree.

NEEDS & WANTS QUIZ

	Need	Want
Movie/TV streaming subscription	○	○
Groceries	○	○
New shoes	○	○
A place to live	○	○
Another car	○	○
Utilities: electricity, gas, water, etc.	○	○
New clothes	○	○
A cruise vacation	○	○
Lawn care service	○	○
Car wash	○	○
Childcare/day care	○	○
Going out to eat every day	○	○
Concert or game tickets	○	○
Auto insurance	○	○
Newest cell phone available	○	○
Premium pet food	○	○
Current cell phone plan	○	○
Gym membership	○	○

Respond to the following questions:

1. What is one item on this list that you thought was a need, but is actually a want?

2. How does identifying something as a want versus a need change your spending habits?

DISCUSSION

Discussion (10 minutes)

☐ **Introduce the Discussion on page 82 by saying:**

> All of us spend money on things we don't really need. And that's okay if you've prioritized your budget and it's a planned expense! But it's not okay to bust your budget buying stuff you don't really need and can't afford. You've got to stick to your budget and stay gazelle intense.
>
> Let's dive into this more in our Discussion on page 82.

☐ **Review the discussion questions.**
Ask for a volunteer to read the first discussion question. Take time to discuss and then move to the next question.

Create Interaction and Don't Fear Silence!

Get the discussion started and then let the members take over. There might be silence after you ask a question—that's okay! Give it a few moments. Silence is a powerful motivator. If you need to initiate the discussion, try answering the question and then calling on members by name.

DISCUSSION

Whether you're in a class or online, be honest with your answers and remember to encourage one another!

1. When was the last time you bought something because of a compelling ad on TV or social media? What about the ad made you dip into your wallet?

2. What's the danger of not talking with your spouse before making a major purchase?

3. What's the worst impulse purchase you've ever made? Why was it so bad? How would you do things differently next time?

4. Think about the idea of opportunity cost: *If I spend money on this, then I can't spend it on that*. How does opportunity cost help you prioritize your spending?

5. On a scale of 1–10, with 1 being "terrified" and 10 being "energized," how would you rank your feelings about negotiating? Why?

KEEP THE CONVERSATION GOING!

Answer these questions online in the Financial Peace community!

financialpeace.com

ENDING THE LESSON

Wrap-Up (3 minutes)

- ☐ **Direct members to page 83, then read through the Action Steps.**
- ☐ **Discuss the importance of the next lesson by saying:**

  > The next lesson is one of the most important—and practical—lessons of the entire course. It will help you make the right choices when it comes to insurance. One mistake in insurance coverage can destroy your entire financial plan. You don't want to miss this lesson!

- ☐ **Reset the room.**
  Return the chairs and clean up the space.

Dismissed!

AFTER THE LESSON

- ☐ **Complete the items on the After Each Lesson checklist on pages 36–37 of this guide.**

ACTION STEPS

It's time to live out what you just learned! Complete each of the Action Steps before the next lesson.

- [ ] **DEFINE YOUR MAJOR PURCHASES**

  What's a "major purchase" in your world? Put a number to it! Singles, run this by your accountability partner to get their feedback. Married couples, decide on this number together.

- [ ] **GET A BETTER DEAL**

  Don't just settle for regular retail outlets. Get creative and find some places where you could get the same thing cheaper: flea market, discount store, scratch/dent store, or resale shop. Identify five things you regularly purchase. How could you find them cheaper?

- [ ] **SET SOCIAL MEDIA LIMITS**

  Wise spending has a lot to do with contentment, and contentment can have a lot to do with what you see on social media. This week, take some practical steps toward limiting social media's negative impact. Try to avoid social media when you first wake up and choose one day to *completely* unplug.

- [ ] **READ *NEGOTIATE A WIN-WIN* ON THE NEXT PAGE**

  If you've never tried to wheel and deal before, negotiating can seem intimidating—but it doesn't have to be! Now that you're armed with our seven negotiating tips, read on for the confidence boost you need to get the deal you want.

NEGOTIATE A WIN-WIN

Everybody wants to get a good deal. That's the happy ending to the spending story, right?

But it can be hard when it seems like everyone is trying to sell you something, and they're just out to get your money. So how can you get the things you need, the things you really want, and still stay on track and on budget?

You negotiate.

If you're immediately intimidated or offended by that word, check out this negotiation story from one of our *Financial Peace University* members! She hits at least four of the seven tips Rachel talks about.

BETHANY WHEELS AND DEALS

“For the past several years, my jobs had always included a company car. When we decided to move to Nashville, that meant giving up the company car and getting my own—super intimidating since neither my husband nor I had ever negotiated anything, let alone a car.

USE THE POWER OF CASH.

We had saved up money to pay cash for the car and our budget was around $10,000. We went to a local car lot (known for great prices and quality cars) and were immediately approached by a salesperson who asked us what we wanted and what our budget was. We hadn't looked at any particular cars before we got there so we were open to most anything.

UNDERSTAND WALK-AWAY POWER.

We weren't jazzed about anything on the lot, and then I eyed a black SUV that was listed at $12,500—clearly over budget. I test-drove it and loved it but tried my best not to get too excited. The biggest key to negotiating is being content to walk away.

IDENTIFY THE GOOD GUY, BAD GUY TECHNIQUE.

We noticed that the tires were going to need to be replaced soon, and it would need the usual 100,000-mile maintenance. With that in mind, we lowballed and made an offer of $7,500—in cash. The salesperson was "on our side" but said he couldn't take that offer to the manager.

SAY, "THAT'S NOT GOOD ENOUGH!"

We came up to $8,000 and the manager offered to give it to us for $12,000 if we financed—big nope. We reiterated that we were paying cash and told them the $500 off wasn't good enough. After a couple more go-rounds, we made a final offer of $9,800, fees and licensing included.

USE WALK-AWAY POWER.

He said no, so we thanked him, and with a little grit, walked away. As we were approaching our car, the manager ran out and we hear, "$10,000 if you finance!"

We were mainly just annoyed at that point, so we had no trouble driving away in the car we showed up in.

We let it go and planned on going to another lot once we moved. But we got a text the next morning from the salesperson asking us to come back. They offered us $9,100 plus licensing and fees. We accepted. Total cost: $10,101. BOOM!

We wrote the check, drove it off the lot, and moved to Nashville the next morning. And that's what we call the power of negotiation.

— BETHANY

Score a deal!

You may not always get a bargain like Bethany. Sometimes, the seller won't budge. Sometimes, when you walk away, the seller will let you. But most times, if you want to negotiate, the seller is willing! Because when you buy a *deal* and they leave with a *sale*, that's what we call a **win-win**.

LESSON 06

THE ROLE OF INSURANCE

LESSON PREP

- Grab a box of tissues—seriously, you may want to bring tissues for your members. If you've already watched the video, you know that parts of this lesson are very powerful. It's not uncommon for some class members to be emotional.
- The topics of life insurance and wills often make people uncomfortable. While it's not the most fun thing to talk about, both are essential to a solid financial plan. Remind everyone eighteen and older that they need a will!
- It's natural for people to have a lot of tactical questions coming out of this lesson. As part of the Action Steps, they'll use the Coverage Checkup tool on financialpeace.com to figure out what they need (and don't need), which questions to ask, and where to get the best coverage.

START THE LESSON

Welcome and Review (3 minutes)

☐ **Welcome class members back.**

☐ **Have a budget checkup!**
Discuss the following questions:

> What impulse purchases did you make, or avoid, since the last lesson?
>
> Which categories are still giving you trouble in your budgets?

- ☐ **Review the Action Steps from the previous lesson.**
  Check to make sure class members completed the Action Steps from Lesson 5. Address any questions or concerns they may have.

Get Ready for the Video

- ☐ **Introduce the video by saying:**

> Most of us avoid talking about insurance. It's boring, it seems expensive, it feels complicated, and, honestly, some people think it's a waste of money. That's why this lesson is so great—you'll leave here with a clear game plan. You'll learn what you need, what you don't need, and how to get it. But since insurance needs change from person to person, make sure to write down any questions you have as you watch the video.
>
> Turn to page 88 and think about this: Why do so many people have negative feelings about insurance?

Start the Video

As the Video Plays

Update your attendance on financialpeace.com or pass around the attendance sheet. Then, follow along with your members in your Coordinator Guide.

LESSON 06

"INSURANCE **PROTECTS** the things that will **MAKE YOU** *wealthy.*"

—DAVE RAMSEY

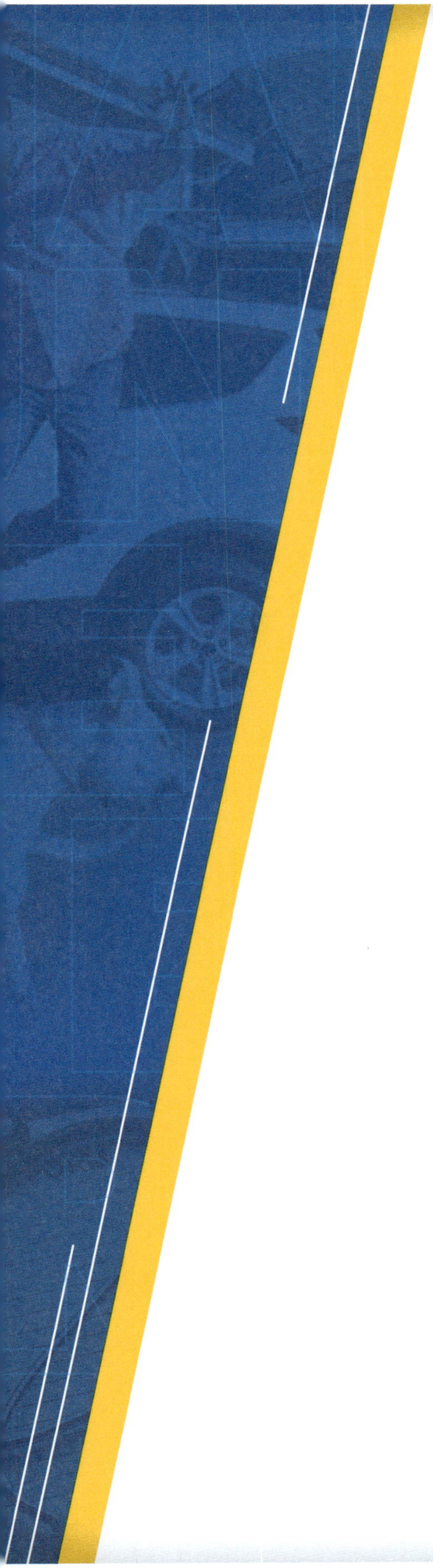

THE ROLE OF INSURANCE

KEY POINTS

The purpose of insurance is simply to transfer risk—this is your defensive game plan.

There are seven basic insurances you actually need.

No exceptions and no excuses, everyone eighteen and older needs a written will.

GUIDE
Dave Ramsey

AUTO INSURANCE

If you have a full emergency fund, raise your ___DEDUCTIBLE___.

Carry adequate ___LIABILITY___.

Consider dropping your ___COLLISION___ on older cars.

HOMEOWNER'S AND RENTER'S INSURANCE

Homeowner's coverage should be guaranteed ___REPLACEMENT___ cost if at all possible.

If you're in an apartment or other rental arrangement, you need ___RENTER'S___ insurance.

An ___UMBRELLA___ liability policy is a good buy once you begin building wealth.

> "THE PURPOSE OF INSURANCE IS *to transfer risk.*"
>
> —DAVE RAMSEY

ANSWER KEY

Deductible
Liability
Collision
Replacement
Renter's
Umbrella

Notes

HEALTH INSURANCE

Increase your deductible and/or coinsurance amount to bring ___PREMIUMS___ down.

Increase your ___STOP___-___LOSS___ but never decrease the ___MAXIMUM___ pay.

The HSA (Health Savings Account) is a ___TAX___-___SHELTERED___ savings account for medical expenses that works with a high-deductible insurance policy.

ANSWER KEY

Premiums
Stop-Loss
Maximum
Tax-Sheltered

DISABILITY INSURANCE

Disability insurance replaces lost ___INCOME___ due to a short-term or permanent disability.

Try to buy disability insurance that pays if you cannot perform the job that you were educated or trained to do. That is called ___OCCUPATIONAL___, or "own occ," disability.

Beware of ___SHORT___-term policies covering less than five years.

Your coverage should be for ___65%___ of your current income.

A ___LONGER___ elimination period will ___LOWER___ your premium cost.

9 mo. elimination
180 lower cost

> WHEREAS YOU DO NOT KNOW WHAT WILL
> **HAPPEN TOMORROW.**
> *For what is your life?*
> IT IS EVEN A VAPOR THAT APPEARS
> FOR A LITTLE TIME AND THEN VANISHES AWAY.
>
> JAMES 4:14 (NKJV)

ANSWER KEY

Income
Occupational
Short
65%
Longer
Lower

* Notes Buy disability insurance w/after tax dollars.

LONG-TERM CARE INSURANCE

Long-term care insurance is for ___NURSING___ home, assisted living facilities, and in-home care.

This is a must-have for anyone ___60___ years old or older.

IDENTITY THEFT PROTECTION

Don't buy ID theft protection that only provides credit report ___MONITORING___.

Good protection includes ___RESTORATION___ services that assign a counselor to clean up the mess.

ANSWER KEY

Nursing
60
Monitoring
Restoration

LIFE INSURANCE

Life insurance is to replace lost income due to **DEATH**.

5 yr
10 yr
20 yr

→ **TERM** insurance is for a specified period, is substantially cheaper, and has no savings plan built into it.

whole Life

CASH **VALUE** insurance is normally for life and is more expensive in order to fund a savings plan.

You need about **10** times your income. Invested at a 10–12% rate of return, the growth would replace your lost income.

Don't forget your **SPOUSE**.

Children only need enough for **BURIAL** expenses.

Notes

ANSWER KEY

Death
Term
Cash Value
10
Spouse
Burial

> "NEVER DO INVESTMENT-TYPE *insurance.*"
>
> —DAVE RAMSEY

INSURANCE TO AVOID

- Credit life and disability
- Cancer and hospital indemnity
- Accidental death
- Prepaid burial policies
- Mortgage life insurance
- Policies with fancy options: return of premium and waiver of premium

Get a written ___WILL___.

Pssst...

When the One-Minute Takeaway appears on the video, that's your cue to move toward the front of the room and kick off this lesson's Activity. Turn the page to prepare for what happens next.

one-minute **TAKEAWAY**

____

____

____

____

____

ANSWER KEY

Will

ACTIVITY

When the Video Ends

☐ **After the One-Minute Takeaway, say:**

> That story is so powerful. How does that story make you think differently about life insurance?

☐ **Wait for the class to respond, then say:**

> The key takeaway from this lesson is that insurance transfers risk you can't afford to cover on your own. When you understand that, it changes how you look at insurance. Let's work through a case study on auto insurance to help us understand why it's so important to have the right coverage.

Activity: Buy the Right Coverage (5 minutes)

☐ **Break members into small groups and introduce the case study on page 94 by saying:**

> Have one person in your group read the Activity on page 94 out loud. Then, take a few minutes to complete the Activity together. I'll be walking around the room if you need help.

- [ ] **After a few minutes, ask for the results of the case study.**
See below for answers:

Answer: In the top scenario with the 25/50/15 policy, Luke will have to pay $90,000 after the insurance covers their part. With this policy, the insurance company only pays up to $25,000 per injured person, up to $50,000 per accident, and up to $15,000 for property damage. That means Luke is responsible for $5,000 for the driver, $50,000 for the passenger, and $35,000 for the other driver's car.

In the next scenario, the second line reflects what the insurance company would pay under a 100/300/100 policy. With this policy, the insurance company pays up to $100,000 per injured person with a maximum of $300,000 per accident, and up to $100,000 for property damage. That means insurance covers all costs! With the 100/300/100 policy, Luke would pay nothing on the third line.

- [ ] **Instruct a volunteer to read the question at the end of the case study.**
Discuss whether the cheaper policy was better for Luke or not.

- [ ] **Encourage members to check their policies by saying:**

> Based on this case study, raise your hand if you're going to check your auto insurance coverage when you get home. I would if I were you! And I'd check all my other policies as well. In fact, to help you, there's a Coverage Checkup tool at financialpeace.com that you'll use as part of your Action Steps for this lesson.

When the Activity Ends

- [ ] **Turn to page 158 of this guide for instructions on how to lead your class through the discussion questions.**

BUY THE RIGHT *Coverage*

AUTO INSURANCE POLICY

Whether you drive a nice car or a beater, you want to make sure you're covered in case life decides to hit you . . . or your car. This is not the time to go cheap on your insurance policy! Work through Luke's scenario to find out why.

Luke's working the Baby Steps and wants to save money wherever he can. So, he gets the state minimum 25/50/15 liability policy.

25 | 50 | 15

25

COVERS INJURIES TO INDIVIDUALS

The maximum amount (in thousands of dollars) **per person** that will be covered

50

COVERS THE TOTAL OF ALL INJURIES TO PEOPLE

The maximum amount (in thousands of dollars) **per accident** that will be covered

15

COVERS DAMAGE TO PROPERTY

The maximum amount (in thousands of dollars) **per accident** that will be covered

ON HIS WAY TO WORK, LUKE HITS A CAR.

The driver of the other car experiences **$30,000** in injury costs and the passenger experiences **$75,000** in injury costs. Luke totals his car and the **$50,000** car of the other driver. Determine how much Luke will have to pay *after* his insurance pays their portion for each of the following.

25/50/15	DRIVER	PASSENGER	DRIVER'S CAR
TOTAL COST OF ACCIDENT	$ 30,000	$ 75,000	$ 50,000
25/50/15 INSURANCE PAYS	– $ 25,000	– $ 25,000	– $ 15,000
LUKE PAYS	= $ 5,000	= $ 50,000	= $ 35,000
		LUKE HAS TO PAY:	$ 90,000

Maxes at $50k (driver and passenger)

And this doesn't even include the cost to replace his own car!

Now, work the same scenario, but this time Luke has a good **100/300/100** insurance policy.

100/300/100	DRIVER	PASSENGER	DRIVER'S CAR
TOTAL COST OF ACCIDENT	$ 30,000	$ 75,000	$ 50,000
100/300/100 INSURANCE PAYS	– $ 30,000	– $ 75,000	– $ 50,000
LUKE PAYS	= $ 0	= $ 0	= $ 0
		LUKE HAS TO PAY:	$ 0

Maxes at $300k (driver and passenger)

(of course, he still has to replace his own car.)

Respond to the following questions:

1. Was the cheaper liability policy (25/50/15) a good choice for Luke? Why or why not?

DISCUSSION

Discussion (8 minutes)

- ☐ **Review the discussion questions.**
  Ask for a volunteer to read the first discussion question on page 96.

- ☐ **Get them engaged!**
  Give members a chance to share their responses. Then continue through the list of questions, letting a different member read each question.

Create Interaction and Don't Fear Silence!

Get the discussion started and then let the members take over. There might be silence after you ask a question—that's okay! Give it a few moments. Silence is a powerful motivator. If you need to initiate the discussion, try answering the question and then calling on members by name.

DISCUSSION

Whether you're in a class or online, be honest with your answers and remember to encourage one another!

1. When have you let the *cost* of insurance dictate how *much* insurance you get in a certain policy? How does this lesson challenge you to think differently?

2. How do you see your fully funded emergency fund fitting into your insurance plan? How can you make sure you have the right balance between the two?

3. Everyone eighteen and over needs a will. Do you have a will? If not, what has been holding you back from getting one?

4. Can you imagine building wealth to the point where you can self-insure? Why or why not? How have the Baby Steps moved you closer to making that a reality?

KEEP THE CONVERSATION GOING!

Answer these questions online in the Financial Peace community!

financialpeace.com

ENDING THE LESSON

Wrap-Up (3 minutes)

- ☐ **Direct members to page 97 and read through the Action Steps.** Then say:

  No matter which Baby Step you're on, *everyone* can do these Action Steps before the next lesson!

- ☐ **Remind class members of the value of their membership by saying:**

  Don't forget that with your Financial Peace membership, you can use the Coverage Checkup tool and find an Endorsed Local Provider who could potentially save you hundreds of dollars on insurance each year.

- ☐ **Stress the importance of the next lesson on investing by saying:**

  The next lesson is all about investing. Even if you're not ready for Baby Step 4, don't skip this lesson! The information will help you make sure you're ready when the time comes. Plus, it will keep you motivated to get through the first three Baby Steps as fast as you can!

- ☐ **Return the chairs and clean up the space.**

Dismissed!

AFTER THE LESSON

- ☐ **Complete the items on the After Each Lesson checklist on pages 36–37 of this guide.**

ACTION STEPS

It's time to live out what you just learned! Complete each of the Action Steps before the next lesson.

- [ ] **REVIEW ALL OF YOUR COVERAGE**
  Take our 5-minute Coverage Checkup on **financialpeace.com** to see where you need to make adjustments to your insurance plan. We'll give you a prioritized list of what to add, drop, or tweak. This includes your will! Then we'll connect you with the service providers we recommend to knock out each item on the list—one and *done*!

- [ ] **LOOK INTO GETTING AN HSA**
  A good Health Savings Account (HSA) can become a "medical envelope" for you and your family. But you need to do a little research to make sure it fits your situation. Talk with your employer about what your company might offer.

- [ ] **READ *TERM LIFE INSURANCE—THE WAY TO GO* ON THE NEXT PAGE**
  You know we're not too big on whole life insurance. In fact, we hate it. But we do recommend you get term life insurance. Read on to learn what you need and why!

Term Life INSURANCE

THE WAY TO GO

Life happens, and without being too morbid, so does unexpected death. We want you to have peace of mind knowing your family will be taken care of when you're gone.

It doesn't matter if you're newly married or heading into retirement. If someone depends on your income, you need life insurance. Plain and simple.

WHOLE LIFE vs. TERM LIFE INSURANCE

There are several types of life insurance—term, whole life, or any kind of cash value life insurance. Term is straightforward, inexpensive, and protects your family. The other ones? Total rip-offs.

1. **Whole life insurance** often costs hundreds of dollars more a month and includes a "savings" plan with a terrible return. Instead, opt for term life. You'll pay a fraction of the price. Then just invest the difference in what you would have paid for whole life insurance.

2. **Term life insurance** is the easiest and least expensive way to protect your family's finances after you're gone. Simply put, here's how term life insurance works: if you or your spouse passes away at any time during this term, your beneficiaries will receive a payout from the policy.

HOW LONG DO I NEED COVERAGE?

Dave's general rule is to buy based on when your kids will be heading off to college and living on their own. Typical terms are 10, 15, 20, or 30 years. **We recommend a 15- or 20-year term.**

Have a newborn in the house? Pick up a 20-year plan. If you have a 10-year-old, a 15-year plan would be a better option for you.

HOW MUCH COVERAGE DO I NEED?

That small policy you're getting through work, which might be one year's worth of coverage, isn't near enough. Always buy a policy that covers **10–12 times your annual pretax income.**

With a good term life policy, by investing the insurance proceeds, your beneficiaries can earn a rate of return that replaces your lost earnings and provides security for your family after you're gone.

Here's what we mean. Let's say you make $40,000. That means you should carry at least $400,000 in coverage.

If your surviving spouse invests that $400,000 in good mutual funds with an average 11% return, they could peel off $44,000 a year from that investment to replace your income without ever cutting into the original investment amount. That's what we call real security.

Get the Right Coverage Today

Simply put, life insurance has one job: it replaces your income when you die.

We hope you'll never have to use it, but the truth is we can't see the future and we aren't promised tomorrow. So the ideal time to buy life insurance is today! Take our **5-minute Coverage Checkup on financialpeace.com** to get the best term life insurance policy for your family.

LESSON 07

RETIREMENT PLANNING

LESSON PREP

- Most members won't be ready to start investing yet. Encourage them to use this long-term goal as motivation to keep up their gazelle intensity and move through Baby Steps 1–3 as fast as they can! Remind them that they can re-watch this lesson later as part of their membership.
- The Activity in this lesson requires some calculations, so bring a calculator or two if you have them. Otherwise, members can use their smartphones.

START THE LESSON

Welcome and Review (5 minutes)

☐ **Welcome class members back by saying:**

> Welcome to Lesson 7! In Lesson 4, we learned about the power of compound interest with Jack and Blake. In this lesson, we'll take a deep dive into investing so you're ready when the time comes for *you* to start investing. I know you all want to start investing right away, but remember to work the Baby Steps in order. You'll be on Baby Step 4 in no time.

- [ ] **Have a budget checkup!**
  Discuss the following question:

  > Everyone should have a *Personal* line item in their budget each month. This is money to use at *your* discretion. How has this helped you stick to your budget?

- [ ] **Review the Action Steps from the previous lesson.**
  Check to make sure class members completed the Action Steps from Lesson 6. Address any questions or concerns they may have.

Get Ready for the Video

- [ ] **Introduce the video by saying:**

  > For most of us, investing can feel really intimidating. In this lesson, Dave will help you understand the basics of investing and how to start investing the right way. As I get ready to start the video, turn to page 102 and think about this: What do the terms *401(k)* and *Roth IRA* mean to you?

Start the Video

As the Video Plays

Update your attendance on financialpeace.com or pass around the attendance sheet. Then, follow along with your members in your Coordinator Guide.

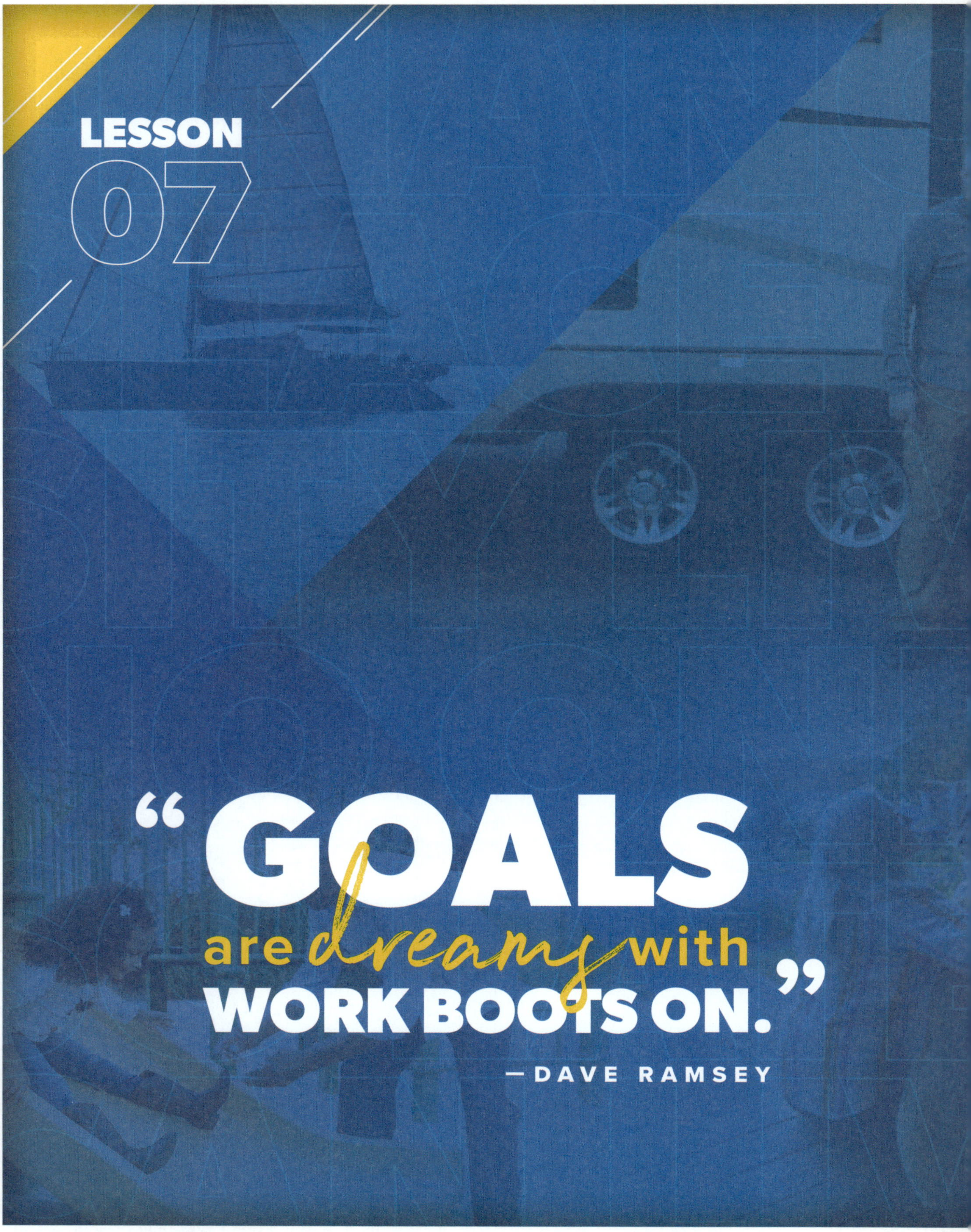

LESSON 07

"GOALS are *dreams* with WORK BOOTS ON."

—DAVE RAMSEY

RETIREMENT PLANNING

KEY POINTS

Investing doesn't have to be complicated. Use the KISS rule: Keep It Simple, Stupid.

Never invest in things you don't understand.

The best way to build wealth is slowly and consistently over time.

LESSON 7 //
RETIREMENT PLANNING

Baby Step 4

GUIDE
Dave Ramsey

Get rid Debt
Emergency
fund in place

29% have less
than $1000 saved
for retirement

GROUND RULES FOR INVESTING

Baby Step 4 is to invest **15%** of your household income into Roth IRAs and pretax retirement plans.

The KISS Rule of Investing: Keep it **SIMPLE**, stupid.

Diversification **LOWERS** risk.

↘ Spread around

> "INVEST IN SEVEN VENTURES, YES, IN EIGHT; **YOU DO NOT KNOW** WHAT DISASTER MAY COME UPON *the land.*"
>
> ECCLESIASTES 11:2 (NIV)

MUTUAL FUNDS

MUTUAL **FUNDS** are where investors pool their money to invest. At least 5 yrs.

Your return comes as the **VALUE** of the fund is increased.

Mutual funds are good for **LONG**-**TERM** investments.

ANSWER KEY

15%
Simple
Lowers
Mutual Funds
Value
Long-Term

Notes Check website often for updates on investing

USE TAX-FAVORED PLANS

Tax-favored means the investment is in a ___QUALIFIED___ ___PLAN___ or has a special tax treatment.

QUALIFIED PLANS

- Individual Retirement Arrangement (IRA)
- 401(k)
- 403(b)
- 457
- Simplified Employee Pension Plan

ANSWER KEY
Qualified Plan

INDIVIDUAL RETIREMENT ARRANGEMENT (IRA)

Remember, an IRA is the tax ___TREATMENT___ on virtually any type of investment. It is *not* a type of investment at a bank.

ROTH IRA

The Roth IRA is an after-tax IRA that grows tax-___FREE___.

> "IF YOU WANT TO BE A MILLIONAIRE, FIGURE OUT WHAT MILLIONAIRES DO AND START DOING IT. *Then you'll get to be one.*"
>
> —DAVE RAMSEY

401(K), 403(B), AND 457 RETIREMENT PLANS

Some companies are now offering the ___ROTH___ 401(k), which grows tax-free.

You should be funding your plan whether your company ___MATCHES___ or not, but the plans that have company matching provide great returns.

ANSWER KEY

Treatment
Free
Roth
Matches

Notes

ROLLOVERS

You should ___ALWAYS___ roll all retirement plans to an IRA when you leave a company.

Don't bring the money home! Make it a ___DIRECT___ transfer.

RETIREMENT LOANS

Never ___BORROW___ on your retirement plan.

ANSWER KEY

Always
Direct
Borrow

OUR SUGGESTION FOR INVESTING 15%

Fund a 401(k) of other employer plans if they match. Fund an amount ___EQUAL___ to the match.

Above the match amount, fund ___ROTH___ IRAs. If there is no match, start with Roth IRAs.

Complete the 15% of your income by going back to the ___401(K)___ or other company plans.

Baby Step #4
Fund through match
Roth IRA

BUILDING WEALTH

The ___TORTOISE___ wins every time.

So, 15% of your income going into retirement isn't for one month or one year. It's for the rest of your ___LIFE___.

Pssst...

When the One-Minute Takeaway appears on the video, that's your cue to move toward the front of the room and kick off this lesson's Activity. See the next page to prepare for what happens next.

one-minute **TAKEAWAY**

ANSWER KEY

Equal
Roth
401(k)
Tortoise
Life

ACTIVITY

When the Video Ends

- ☐ **After the One-Minute Takeaway, say:**

  Until now, we've been looking at other people's numbers during our activities. In today's Activity, you'll be using your own numbers to see what investing early can do for your retirement. If you have a calculator on your phone, you may need it.

- ☐ **Turn the page for instructions on leading your class through the Activity.**

ACTIVITY

Activity: What Could Your Money Turn Into? (8 minutes)

☐ **Introduce the Activity on page 107 by saying:**

> Everyone turn to page 107 and take a few minutes to work through the Activity. Married couples, work on this together. I'll be walking around the room if you need help.

☐ **After a few minutes, check that members completed the Activity.** See below for answers:

Answer: Your monthly gross income is what you make before taxes each month. If you're a two-income family, include both incomes in this Activity.

Multiply your monthly income by 15%, which is .15 on your calculator. That will tell you how much you should be investing each month if you were on Baby Step 4 right now. For example, if your monthly gross income is $5,000 ($60,000/yr), 15% would be a $750 monthly contribution.

You can compare that number to the Monthly Contribution chart to see where you could be in 20, 30, or 40 years.

☐ **After the Activity, discuss the two follow-up questions as a class.**

When the Activity Ends

☐ **Turn to page 176 of this guide for instructions on how to lead your class through the discussion questions.**

WHAT COULD YOUR MONEY *Turn Into?*

Your most powerful wealth-building tool is your income—until your investments start earning more than you do. That's why you want to get to **Baby Step 4** as fast as you can!

Take your current monthly gross income and calculate how much you would invest if you were on Baby Step 4 right now.

ON BABY STEP 4, I WOULD NEED TO INVEST:

$	x	.15	=	
MONTHLY GROSS INCOME		15 PERCENT		MONTHLY CONTRIBUTION

Before the next lesson, you'll go to **financialpeace.com** and use the Investment Calculator to see exactly what your monthly investment could look like in **20, 30, and 40 years** at an 11% rate of return!

For now, check out the table below to get ballpark numbers.

MONTHLY CONTRIBUTION	20 YEARS	30 YEARS	40 YEARS
$700	$611,501	$1,981,159	$6,075,272
$800	$698,858	$2,264,182	$6,943,168
$900	$786,215	$2,547,205	$7,811,067

Respond to the following questions:

1. What comes to mind when you see what your monthly investment could turn into?

2. How do you feel knowing that if your income increases, you'll get to invest even *more* each month?

DISCUSSION

Discussion (8 minutes)

- ☐ **Review the discussion questions.**
  Ask a volunteer to read the first question on page 108 in the Member Workbook. Take time to discuss, then move to the next question.

Create Interaction and Don't Fear Silence!

Get the discussion started and then let the members take over. There might be silence after you ask a question—that's okay! Give it a few moments. Silence is a powerful motivator. If you need to initiate the discussion, try answering the question and then call on members by name.

DISCUSSION

Whether you're in a class or online, be honest with your answers and remember to encourage one another!

1. If the stock market goes up, keep investing. If the stock market goes down, guess what? You keep investing! Dave says the only people who get hurt on a roller coaster are the ones who try to jump off midway. What has always made you nervous about investing? How has what you learned in this lesson calmed some of those fears?

2. What are some of the big problems with investments like gold, certificates of deposits, single stocks, and bonds? What should you do if you're investing in them right now?

3. Investing is the key to building wealth, and building wealth is the key to creating a legacy that will outlive you. How do you want to set your family up for success after you're gone?

4. Right now, are you the tortoise or the hare? What should you be doing to make sure you always win with investing?

KEEP THE CONVERSATION GOING!

Answer these questions online in the Financial Peace community!

financialpeace.com

ENDING THE LESSON

Wrap-Up (3 minutes)

- ☐ **Direct members to page 109, then read through the Action Steps.**
- ☐ **Stress the importance of the next lesson by saying:**

  Can you imagine what it would feel like to not have any debt, including your mortgage? In the next lesson, you'll learn everything you need to know about real estate and mortgages. Don't miss it!

- ☐ **Reset the room.**
  Return the chairs and clean up the space.

Dismissed!

AFTER THE LESSON

- ☐ **Complete the items on the After Each Lesson checklist on pages 36–37 of this guide.**
- ☐ **Start thinking about your final lesson!**
  Many coordinators plan a celebration for the final lesson. It's time to start thinking about what you want to do so you can announce it in your next lesson. Check out the Resources section of your Coordinator Dashboard for a list of celebration ideas!

ACTION STEPS

It's time to live out what you just learned! Complete each of the Action Steps before the next lesson.

☐ USE THE INVESTMENT CALCULATOR

In the Activity, you calculated 15% of your monthly income that will go into retirement savings. Ready to see what that number could become in 20, 30, and 40 years? Use the Investment Calculator at **financialpeace.com** to see what your monthly investment could turn into!

☐ SPREAD THAT MONEY AROUND

In this lesson, you learned about diversification—spreading money around so it will grow. You want to keep your risk low and your reward high! If you're ready for Baby Step 4, go to **financialpeace.com** to connect with a SmartVestor Pro in your area and start investing the right way.

☐ CHECK YOUR GAZELLE INTENSITY

You're seven lessons into *Financial Peace University*, and you're doing great. How are you feeling about your progress? Use the scale below to gauge your gazelle intensity.

1 2 3 4 5 6 7 8 9 10

RUNNING SLOW ⟷ **STARVING THE CHEETAH!**

If you're at a 10, great work! If you're running a little slow, what's one thing you can do this week to amp up your intensity?

☐ READ *MUTUAL FUNDS 101* ON THE NEXT PAGE

Investing isn't one-size-fits-all. Because you never invest in something you don't understand, you need to learn what's best for you. Read on for a crash course on mutual funds!

MUTUAL FUNDS 101

If you want to win with money, find someone who's won with money and copy them. If you want to build wealth, find someone who's wealthy and copy them! The good news is we found 10,000 of them for you.

In our research for Chris Hogan's book *Everyday Millionaires: How Ordinary People Built Extraordinary Wealth—and How You Can Too*, we surveyed over 10,000 millionaires and asked them how they built their wealth. The number one answer? By investing early and consistently in their company 401(k) plans.

That's why we do **Baby Step 4**: Invest 15% of your household income in retirement.

When you're ready to start investing, you won't need to camp out on the trading floor of the New York Stock Exchange. Just keep it simple and follow the investing advice that's worked for over 20 years!

Invest in the right mix of **mutual funds** with a history of strong performance and stick with them over time.

THE 4 TYPES OF MUTUAL FUNDS *You Should Use!*

GROWTH

Growth funds are some of the most common types of mutual funds. Using mid-cap funds (cap is short for capitalization, or money), they generally include medium-sized companies that are still growing—and still making money. Growth funds can provide above-average growth for your money with above-average risk. Over the long run though, they live up to their name: growth funds.

GROWTH AND INCOME

Dave calls these "obedient, predictable child" funds. They include large-cap funds with a lot of big-name companies you probably recognize. Growth and income funds usually grow steadily with an average risk. So, you won't make a fortune overnight, but you won't lose it all either.

AGGRESSIVE GROWTH

Dave calls these "wild child" funds. They can have an incredible return one year, then lose money the next. A small-cap fund is one example of an aggressive growth fund. These funds are generally made up of smaller, active, emerging companies, such as start-ups and tech companies. They have the potential for a higher return—but also carry greater risk.

INTERNATIONAL

International funds invest in companies outside the United States. But they still might be companies you recognize. That's because so many products created in the United States are actually owned by international companies. International funds carry varying degrees of risk, but they're great for diversification.

Let us help!

Investing doesn't have to be intimidating. A SmartVestor Pro can help you invest the right way. Find these investing professionals in your area at **financialpeace.com**.

LESSON 08

REAL ESTATE & MORTGAGES

LESSON PREP

- In this lesson, Dave recommends a 15-year fixed-rate mortgage (if you can't put 100% down on a home). Keep in mind that most of your class will already have a 30-year mortgage if they own a home.
- After this lesson, some members may be ready to buy a home. Direct them to financialpeace.com to connect with a real estate Endorsed Local Provider. (This is part of their Action Steps!)
- Be ready to discuss the details of the celebration you have planned for Lesson 9.

START THE LESSON

Welcome and Review (5 minutes)

☐ **Welcome class members back by saying:**

> Welcome back, everyone! We're eight lessons in, so let's take a minute and celebrate some wins:
>
> Has anyone moved forward in the Baby Steps since Lesson 1?

If anyone raises their hand, ask which Baby Step they started on and which Baby Step they're on now. Celebrate with them!

- ☐ **Have a budget checkup!**
  Discuss the following questions:

  > How has living on a budget been going this week compared to the very first week you started?
  >
  > Is budgeting becoming more of a habit for you? How so?

  > Note: If members are discouraged, remind them that it takes a few months to get the hang of it!

- ☐ **Review the Action Steps from the previous lesson.**
  Check to make sure class members completed the Action Steps from Lesson 7. Address any questions or concerns they may have.

Get Ready for the Video

- ☐ **Introduce the video by saying:**

  > In this lesson, Dave will share from over 30 years of his personal experience in real estate to help you know when and how to rent, buy, and sell a house. As I get ready to start the video, turn to page 114 in your workbooks and think about this: How would it feel to own a completely paid-for home?

Start the Video

As the Video Plays

Update your attendance on financialpeace.com or pass around the attendance sheet. Then, follow along with your members in your Coordinator Guide.

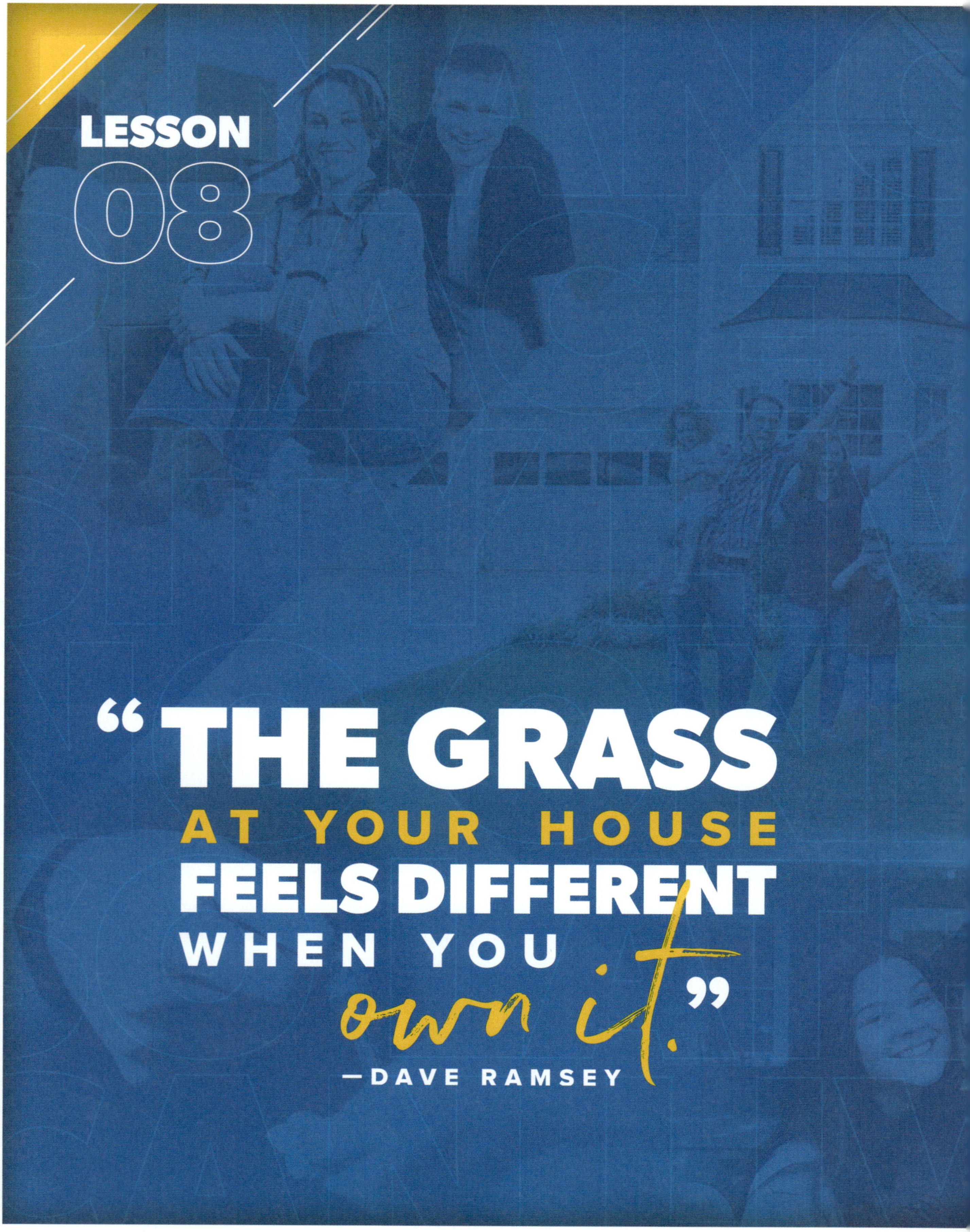

LESSON 08

"THE GRASS AT YOUR HOUSE FEELS DIFFERENT WHEN YOU *own it.*"

—DAVE RAMSEY

REAL ESTATE & MORTGAGES

KEY POINTS

A house is the largest financial investment you will ever make.

Here's your home-buying plan: a 15-year fixed-rate mortgage with at least a 10% down payment, and monthly payments of no more than 25% of your take-home pay.

When you pay off your home, you're 100% debt-free!

GUIDE
Dave Ramsey

RENTING

There is nothing wrong with ___RENTING___ for a little while. This demonstrates patience and wisdom.

WHEN TO BUY

You should be finished with Baby Step 3. That means you are debt-free and have a full emergency fund in place.

WHY TO BUY

- It's a ___FORCED___ savings plan.
- It's an ___INFLATION___ hedge.
- It grows virtually ___TAX___-___FREE___.

Notes

ANSWER KEY

Renting
Forced
Inflation
Tax-Free

Notes

WHAT TO BUY

- Buy in the ___BOTTOM___ price range of the neighborhood, and never overbuild your neighborhood through home additions and improvements.
- Homes appreciate in good neighborhoods and are priced based on three things: location, location, and location.
- If possible, buy near water or with a ___VIEW___.
- Buy bargains by overlooking bad landscaping, ugly carpet, outdated wallpaper, and the Elvis print in the master bedroom.
- Always buy a home that is (or can be) attractive from the street and has a good basic floor plan.

ANSWER KEY

Bottom
View

GUIDE
Chris Hogan

HOW TO BUY

Real estate agents have full access to the ___MULTIPLE___ Listing Service (MLS) and can make house hunting easier.

Always get a land survey if you're buying more than a standard subdivision lot.

Have the home inspected mechanically and structurally by a certified ___HOME___ ___INSPECTOR___. Get an appraisal but understand that it's just an "opinion of value."

Title insurance insures you against an unclean title, which is when your property ownership is called into question. It is a must-buy.

Get a monthly payment of no more than ___25%___ of your take-home pay on a ___15___-___YEAR___ fixed-rate loan, with at least ___10%___ down.

> "AS FOR ME AND MY HOUSE, WE WILL SERVE *the Lord.*"
>
> JOSHUA 24:15 (ESV)

ANSWER KEY

Multiple
Home Inspector
25%
15-year
10%

Notes

HORRIBLE MORTGAGE OPTIONS

- ___ARMs___ or Adjustable-Rate Mortgages
    - The concept of the ARM is to transfer the risk of higher interest rates to the borrower. So, in return, the lender gives a lower rate.
    - If you have an ARM, refinance immediately!
- Interest-only loans are a bad idea because you're only paying the interest.
- ___REVERSE___ Mortgages
- Accelerated or Biweekly Payoff Program

ANSWER KEY

ARMs
Reverse

GUIDE
Dave Ramsey

BASIC WAYS TO FINANCE A HOME

- ___CONVENTIONAL___ loans are usually through Fannie Mae and are privately insured against default.
- PMI is private mortgage insurance.
- ___FHA___ (Federal Housing Administration) loans are insured by HUD—the federal government.
- VA loans are insured by the US Department of Veterans Affairs.
- Owner financing is when you pay the owner over time, making him or her the mortgage holder.

> **“100% OF FORECLOSURES HAPPEN ON HOMES** *with a mortgage.*”
>
> –DAVE RAMSEY

Notes

ANSWER KEY

Conventional
FHA

Notes

CHALLENGES AND OPPORTUNITIES

If you do what we teach, your credit score will eventually hit zero, which means you'll need to find a mortgage lender that does ___MANUAL___ underwriting.

When you owe more on your house than it is currently worth, you are upside down on your home.

In a ___SHORT___ sale, the home is sold for less than the amount owed, and the lienholder agrees to accept the proceeds from the home sale as payment in full without recourse.

Willfully walking away from a mortgage—even though you have the money to make the payments—is called strategic default.

ANSWER KEY

Manual
Short

GUIDE
Dave Ramsey

SELLING A HOME

The most important aspect of preparation is attention to ___CURB___ appeal.

The exposure through the ___MULTIPLE___ Listing Service is worth it.

You should interview at least three real estate agents.

Have your agent do a detailed Comparative Market Analysis (CMA) to accurately price your home.

Pssst...

When the One-Minute Takeaway appears on the video, that's your cue to move toward the front of the room and kick off this lesson's Activity. See the next page to prepare for what happens next.

one-minute **TAKEAWAY**

____

____

____

____

____

____

____

____

____

ANSWER KEY

Curb
Multiple

ACTIVITY

When the Video Ends

- ☐ **After the One-Minute Takeaway, say:**

  You may have learned some things you've never heard before—and some things you wish you knew years ago. Let's dig into a case study to see what kind of impact the right mortgage can have on your finances long term.

- ☐ **Turn the page for instructions on leading your class through the Activity.**

ACTIVITY

Activity: Buy a Home the Right Way (7 minutes)

- ☐ **Introduce the case study on page 121 by saying:**

  Let's turn to page 121 and take a few minutes to read and work through the case study. This is a basic example to help demonstrate how different mortgage options can impact your finances.

- ☐ **After a few minutes, ask for the results of the case study.**

  Answer: Drew and Amy will pay $61,963 more than Charles and Misty.

- ☐ **Ask a volunteer to read question one at the end of the case study.**

  Answer: Charles and Misty. By picking a 15-year fixed-rate mortgage, they end up paying almost $62,000 less for their home. Not to mention they'll have a 15-year head start on Baby Step 7 that Drew and Amy won't have.

- ☐ **Ask a volunteer to read question two at the end of the case study.**

  Possible Answers:
  Add a deck, do some landscaping, finish the basement, upgrade the kitchen, etc.

When the Activity Ends

- ☐ **Turn to page 196 of this guide for instructions on how to lead your class through the discussion questions.**

BUY A HOME *the Right Way*

Drew and Amy and Charles and Misty each put **20%** down on a **$200,000** home at a **4%** annual interest rate.

$200,000 HOME	DREW & AMY	CHARLES & MISTY

MORTGAGE (FIXED)	**30-YEAR**	**15-YEAR**
PAYMENT (MONTHLY)	**$764**	**$1,184**
TOTAL	**$274,993** AFTER 30 YEARS	**$213,030** AFTER 15 YEARS

WHILE DREW & AMY PAY LESS IN THE SHORT TERM, THEY PAY HOW MUCH MORE OVERALL?

$ **$61,963**

(Hint: $274,993–$213,030)

Respond to the following questions:

1. Based on this example, would you rather be Drew and Amy or Charles and Misty? Why?

2. What could Charles and Misty do with the difference to build additional equity in their home? What would *you* do with the difference?

DISCUSSION

Discussion (8 minutes)

- ☐ **Review the discussion questions.**
  Ask a volunteer to read the first question on page 122 in the Member Workbook. Take time to discuss, then move to the next question.

Create Interaction and Don't Fear Silence!

Get the discussion started and then let the members take over. There might be silence after you ask a question—that's okay! Give it a few moments. Silence is a powerful motivator. If you need to initiate the discussion, try answering the question and then calling on members by name.

DISCUSSION

Whether you're in a class or online, be honest with your answers and remember to encourage one another!

1. When you picture your dream home, what do you see? What parts of your home stand out and why are they important to you?

2. Based on what you've learned from Dave and Chris, how do you know if you have too much house?

3. Based on your answer to question two, do you need to make any adjustments to your housing situation? If so, what? Refinance? Sell? Buy? Throw more money at your mortgage?

4. If you're a homeowner, think about life without a mortgage. What could you do with the extra money that's currently going toward payments? If you're renting, how do you feel about owning a home someday? How could you save up for one?

KEEP THE CONVERSATION GOING!

Answer these questions online in the Financial Peace community!

financialpeace.com

ENDING THE LESSON

Wrap-Up (5 minutes)

- ☐ **Direct members to page 123, then read through the Action Steps.**
- ☐ **Challenge class members to finish strong by saying:**

  The next lesson is our very last lesson together! In Lesson 9, you'll learn how to truly live and give like no one else. In fact, you'll learn the key to financial peace. It's an incredible lesson that shows us what this whole course is really about. You don't want to miss our last lesson!

- ☐ **Remind class members to complete their last Financial Snapshot.** They can transfer the information from the Financial Snapshot tool at financialpeace.com to the card found in their Member Workbook.
- ☐ **Share details of your Lesson 9 celebration plans with your class!**
- ☐ **Reset the room and clean up the space.**

Dismissed!

AFTER THE LESSON

- ☐ **Complete the items on the After Each Lesson checklist on pages 36–37 of this guide.**
- ☐ **Get ready for your final lesson!**

ACTION STEPS

It's time to live out what you just learned! Complete each of the Action Steps before the next lesson.

- ☐ **USE THE MORTGAGE CALCULATOR AND CONNECT WITH A REAL ESTATE ELP**
  If you're a homeowner, use the Mortgage Calculator on **financialpeace.com** to figure out how much you're paying in interest over time—and to see how quickly you could pay off your home with extra payments. If you're ready to buy, use the calculator to see how much house you can afford, then connect with a real estate Endorsed Local Provider!

- ☐ **TAKE A LOOK AT YOUR BUDGET**
  As part of your next budget, put some extra focus on your housing category. How much are you assigning to housing? Based on the lesson, do you have too much house?

- ☐ **INVESTIGATE A REFINANCE**
  If you're in a bad mortgage like an adjustable-rate mortgage (ARM), you don't have to stay there—and you shouldn't! Research how to refinance to a 15-year fixed-rate mortgage.

- ☐ **COMPLETE YOUR FINANCIAL SNAPSHOT**
  Now that you've completed eight lessons, use the Financial Snapshot tool at **financialpeace.com** to list your debt paid off, amount saved, and credit cards cut up or closed. If you're in a class, don't forget to transfer that information to your second Financial Snapshot card (page 120) and turn it in to your coordinator at the start of Lesson 9. Celebrate your progress!

- ☐ **READ *PMI: NECESSARY OR NOT?* ON THE NEXT PAGE**
  During the lesson, Chris described what PMI is all about. This article shares a little more about why it's not worth the trouble and how to knock it out once and for all.

LESSON 8 //
DEEP DIVE

PMI: NECESSARY or Not?

We're going to save you $10,000 before this article ends. Ready?

You've worked the Baby Steps, done your research, and kept an eye on the housing market. You're ready to buy a home. If you can't put 100% down, you'll move through a mortgage approval process where you may encounter **private mortgage insurance** (PMI).

Hold on a second. You might be asking yourself, *Was this on the list of the seven insurances I need to have?* We're glad you asked. The answer is no. And here's why.

AT A GLANCE

PMI = **PRIVATE MORTGAGE INSURANCE**

IF YOU PUT 20% DOWN, **YOU AVOID IT**

RATES RANGE FROM **.5–1.5% OF HOME LOAN AMOUNTS**

WHAT IS PMI?

PMI protects the lender. You're about to borrow a lot of money, and your lender wants to make sure they get their money back if you can't make the payments and end up in foreclosure. Every year, there are between 500,000–1.5 million home foreclosures, so you can understand why lenders want insurance. **PMI protects their investment.**

But here's the catch: You're the one who will be paying the insurance premiums—*not* them.

HOW MUCH DOES PMI COST?

PMI rates can range anywhere from .5–1.5% or more of your loan amount. For this example, let's use a 1% PMI and a $200,000 home loan amount.

At 1%, that would make your PMI $2,000 per year—an extra $166.67 per month added to your mortgage payment. After five years, PMI has added **$10,000** to the cost of your home. *There's that $10,000 you can save yourself.*

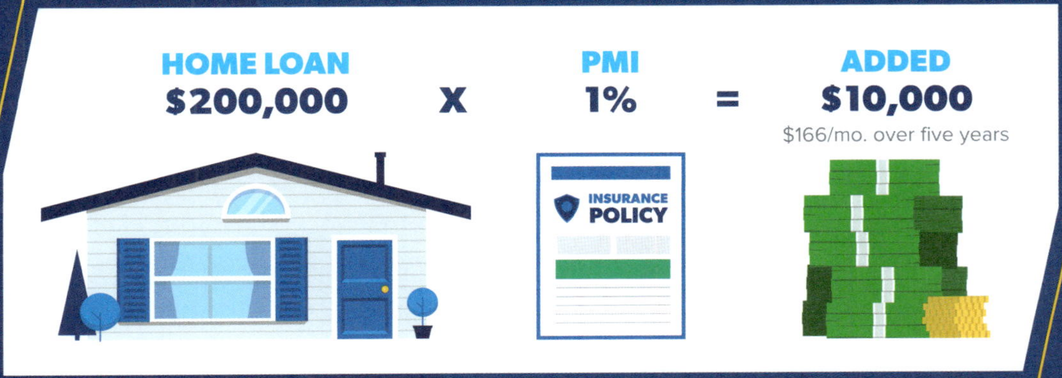

HOW CAN I AVOID PMI?

The easiest way to avoid PMI is to put at least **20% down** on your home. That completely eliminates PMI. If you *don't* put 20% down, PMI will be added to your loan automatically! You won't be able to get rid of it until you've paid down your loan enough to have 20–25% equity in your home. Basically, your loan-to-value amount has to be less than 80%.

HAVE A PLAN AND USE A PROFESSIONAL

If you're going to buy a home and get a mortgage, stick to this plan: Find a real estate agent you trust and get a 15-year fixed-rate mortgage with at least 10% down (though 20% is best), and make sure the total payments (including PMI) are no more than 25% of your take-home pay.

Let us help!

Ready to find a real estate agent you trust?
Go to **financialpeace.com** to find a real estate Endorsed Local Provider in your area who is ready to walk you through the home-buying process.

LESSON 09

OUTRAGEOUS GENEROSITY

LESSON PREP

- Members who have attended at least eight of the nine lessons will be excited to get their graduation certificates. Be sure to print them from your Coordinator Dashboard and bring them with you.
- Some members may forget to bring their Financial Snapshot card. Print extra copies of the card from your Coordinator Dashboard for them.
- Ready to have some serious fun? It's your final lesson! That means it's time to celebrate. If you planned a party, don't forget any food or decorations you'll need.

START THE LESSON

Welcome and Review (5 minutes)

☐ **Express appreciation!**
Let your members know how much you've enjoyed getting to know them. Remind them that even though this is the last lesson, it is NOT the end of their membership. They will continue to have access to financialpeace.com with their active membership.

☐ **Collect the Financial Snapshot cards.**
If anyone forgot their Financial Snapshot card, give them one of the extras you printed. You'll tally up the numbers during the video to share before the Activity.

☐ **Have a budget checkup!**

> Why is it important to make sure you budget every month for the rest of your life?

- [ ] **Review the Action Steps from the previous lesson.**
  Check to make sure class members completed the Action Steps from Lesson 8. Address any questions or concerns they may have.

Get Ready for the Video

- [ ] **Introduce the video by saying:**

> In this lesson, Dave reveals the truth to winning in both life and with money. As I get ready to start the video, turn to page 128 and think about this: What do you want your money to say about your life?

Start the Video

As the Video Plays

- [ ] **Update your class's Financial Snapshot.**
  Add up the information from the Financial Snapshot cards and enter it into your Coordinator Dashboard. You'll share this information with your class when the video ends.

- [ ] **Update your attendance and watch the video.**
  Update your attendance on financialpeace.com or pass around the attendance sheet. Then, follow along with your members in your Coordinator Guide.

LESSON 09

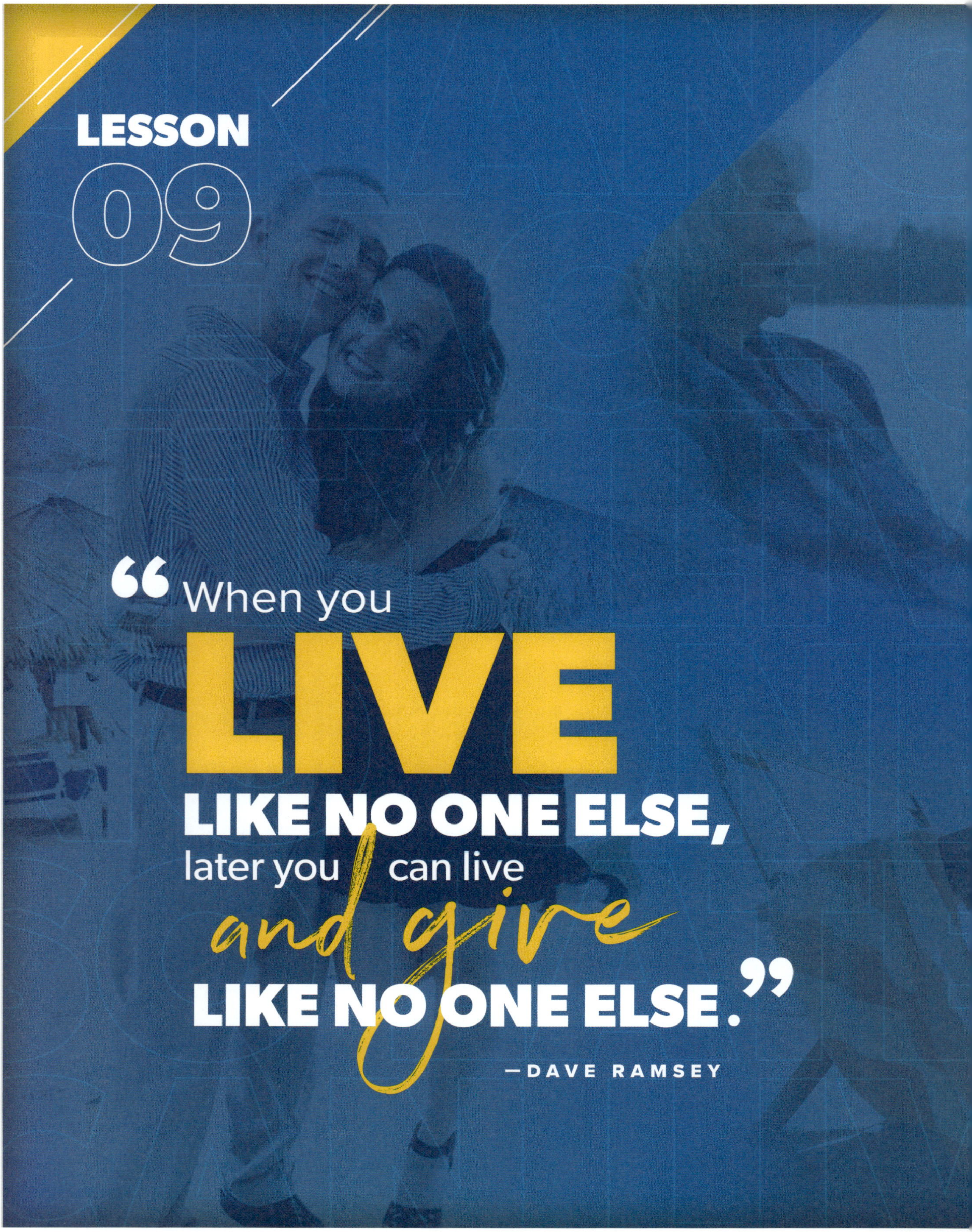

"When you **LIVE** LIKE NO ONE ELSE, later you can live *and give* LIKE NO ONE ELSE."

—DAVE RAMSEY

Life ON THE PLAN

OUTRAGEOUS GENEROSITY

KEY POINTS

If we all became outrageously generous, we could completely change the landscape of America.

God is a giver and because we're made in His image, we are designed to be generous!

God owns it all. We are just managers of His money.

GUIDE
Dave Ramsey

TRUE FINANCIAL PEACE

The ___PEACE___ in financial peace comes from outrageous generosity.

> "You cannot shake hands WITH A CLENCHED FIST."
>
> –INDIRA GANDHI

GIVING CHANGES YOU

We are happiest and most fulfilled when serving and ___GIVING___ .

> "A GENEROUS PERSON WILL PROSPER; WHOEVER REFRESHES OTHERS WILL BE *refreshed*."
>
> PROVERBS 11:25 (NIV)

GENEROSITY COULD CHANGE AMERICA

If "we the people" increased our giving a ___FEW___ percentage points, we could do things like eradicate domestic hunger, fund adoption from foster care, and build hospitals.

WHY GOD TELLS US TO GIVE

The more generous you become, the more you're becoming who God ___MADE___ you to be.

ANSWER KEY

Peace
Giving
Few
Made

Notes

TITHES AND OFFERINGS

The tithe is a ___TENTH___ of your increase.

The Bible says to give your tithe off the ___TOP___ (firstfruits).

The tithe goes to your local ___CHURCH___ .

Offerings are above the tithe and are freely given from ___SURPLUS___ .

"YOU SHALL TRULY *tithe* ALL THE INCREASE OF YOUR GRAIN THAT THE FIELD PRODUCES YEAR BY YEAR."

DEUTERONOMY 14:22 (NKJV)

ANSWER KEY

Tenth
Top
Church
Surplus

OWNERS AND MANAGERS

God owns it all. We are just asset ___MANAGERS___ for the Lord.

> "THE EARTH IS THE LORD'S, AND **THE FULNESS** *thereof.*"
>
> PSALM 24:1 (KJV)

Notes

ANSWER KEY

Managers

DEBT FREEDOM

The Bible calls sin "debt," but Jesus already paid that debt. The only thing you have to do to become debt-free is accept the gift.

> "FOR GOD SO LOVED THE WORLD THAT HE **GAVE HIS ONLY BEGOTTEN SON,** THAT WHOEVER BELIEVES IN HIM SHOULD NOT PERISH BUT HAVE *everlasting life.*"
>
> JOHN 3:16 (NKJV)

Pssst...

When the One-Minute Takeaway appears on the video, that's your cue to move toward the front of the room and kick off this lesson's Activity. Turn the page to prepare for what happens next.

one-minute **TAKEAWAY**

ACTIVITY

When the Video Ends

☐ **After the One-Minute Takeaway, say:**

As Dave said, the peace in financial peace comes from outrageous generosity. Plus, giving is the most fun you can have with money! In today's Activity, you'll get a chance to write down different ways you can start giving. Then we'll look at our class's Financial Snapshot to see the progress we've made since the first lesson.

Activity: Give To Look More Like God (8 minutes)

☐ **Introduce the Activity on page 132 by saying:**

Take a few minutes to work through the Activity on page 132 of your workbook. There are already a couple of examples in each category. Then write down other ways you want to give.

☐ **Allow time for members to complete the Activity, then ask:**

What are some of the ideas you all wrote down?

Which of these ideas can you do this week?

Activity: Financial Snapshot (2 minutes)

- ☐ **Share your class's Financial Snapshot figures. Then say:**

  Can you believe how much you accomplished in just nine lessons? Think of what you'll accomplish in nine months or nine years! And we're just one small class. What would happen if the whole community or even our nation started handling money God's ways? Imagine what we'd be able to do. How much do you think we'd be able to give?

When the Activity Ends

- ☐ **Turn to page 214 of this guide for instructions on how to lead your class through the discussion questions.**

Give to look more LIKE GOD

Giving changes you. We're not trying to be mushy or corny—it's a fact. You see, God is the ultimate giver. And when we give, we start to look more like Him.

1 Chronicles 29:14 (NIV) says, "Everything comes from you, and we have given you only what comes from your hand."

Everything we have comes from God. He owns it all! When He asks us to give, it's not because He needs our money. **His goal is not to reshape economics. His goal is to reshape our hearts.**

When you give your money, your time, and your talents to help and love other people, it doesn't change them as much as it changes you! And God's all about changing *you*. That's what this whole journey toward financial peace is about—changing you.

Remember, the *peace* in financial peace comes from outrageous generosity!

YOU SHOULD *always* BE A GIVER

BABY STEPS 1 2 3 — In Baby Steps 1–3, you might only be giving a tithe to your local church.

BABY STEPS 4 5 6 — In Baby Steps 4–6, you may have a little room in your budget to start giving offerings.

BABY STEP 7 — By the time you hit Baby Step 7, you're giving from your surplus with outrageous generosity!

WAYS YOU CAN START GIVING

Jot down ideas about how you can start giving your money, time, and talents today—no matter which Baby Step you're on!

1 MONEY

Budget a tithe (10% of your income off the top) to your local church.

Give a 100% (or more!) tip at a restaurant.

2 TIME

Volunteer to be a Big Brother/Sister.

Sign up to serve at a local nonprofit or ministry you're passionate about.

3 TALENTS

Lend your skills and volunteer to help build a home.

Put your mechanical talents to work and help fix your neighbor's car.

DISCUSSION

Discussion (8 minutes)

- ☐ **Review the discussion questions.**
  Ask a volunteer to read the first question on page 134 in the Member Workbook. Take time to discuss, then move to the next question.

Create Interaction and Don't Fear Silence!

Get the discussion started and then let the members take over. There might be silence after you ask a question—that's okay! Give it a few moments. Silence is a powerful motivator. If you need to initiate the discussion, try answering the question and then calling on members by name.

DISCUSSION

Whether you're in a class or online, be honest with your answers and remember to encourage one another!

1. Remember, no matter where you are in the Baby Steps, giving should be the priority in your budget! How has this lesson helped you better understand the reason this is so important?

2. Giving is the most fun you can have with money! How have you had fun with giving in the past? What's one way you want to be outrageously generous in the future?

3. What keeps you from giving as much as you'd like to give? How does this lesson help you work through that hang-up?

4. Whether you have a little or a lot, God owns it all! How does His ownership of everything affect the way you think about what He's given you to manage?

KEEP THE CONVERSATION GOING!

Answer these questions online in the Financial Peace community!

financialpeace.com

ENDING THE LESSON

Wrap-Up (15 minutes)

- ☐ **Direct members to page 135, then read through the Action Steps.** Remind members of the importance of completing them after this lesson, even though you won't be meeting again as a class.
- ☐ **Offer a final plasectomy opportunity by saying:**

  > It's the last lesson and we're wrapping up. I've got my scissors here with me! Who wants to start our celebration off right by cutting up their credit cards once and for all?

- ☐ **Celebrate together and hand out graduation certificates!** Share your appreciation for your class. Acknowledge how hard they've worked and encourage them to keep going—because it will be worth it!
- ☐ **Reset the room and clean up the space.**

Dismissed!

AFTER THE LESSON

- ☐ **Complete the items on the After Each Lesson checklist on pages 36–37 of this guide.**
- ☐ **Make sure all of your records are complete for this course.** Check that your attendance and Financial Snapshot figures are up to date.
- ☐ **Encourage class members to become coordinators!** Most volunteer coordinators are former FPU members who want to spread the message of financial peace and help others change their lives. Direct any members who are interested to page 139 in their Member Workbook.

ACTION STEPS

It's time to live out what you just learned! Complete each of the Action Steps below.

☐ **GRATITUDE LEADS YOU TO CONTENTMENT**

Whether you're on Baby Step 2 or 7, God has given you something to manage. Instead of chasing what's next, stop to practice **contentment** and thank God for what He's given you. In the space below, write three things you're thankful for!

1. ______________________________
2. ______________________________
3. ______________________________

☐ **LOOK BACK AND CHARGE AHEAD**

No matter where you are in the Baby Steps, your life should already look different than it did before you started. In the space below, list the top three things you've learned and then list your why—**the reason you refuse to quit**. This is why you won't give up when things get tough, and why you'll live like no one else so later you can live and *give* like no one else.

1. ______________________________
2. ______________________________
3. ______________________________

I will NOT give up because ______________________________

____

☐ **STAY PLUGGED INTO YOUR MEMBERSHIP**

Your Financial Peace membership is the best place to go for motivation and instruction. Log in every week to use tools, watch videos, update your budget, and more!

WELL DONE!

THANKS FOR *Changing* LIVES!

Congratulations on leading a successful class!

You've forever changed the lives of people right in your community. They will never be the same—all because you made the decision to live and give like no one else! Thank you.

When Dave started teaching these principles, he set out on a mission to share the life-change he experienced with as many people as he could. Since then, we've grown so much and helped tens of millions of people. We're honored that YOU chose to join us.

Thank you for giving your time for other people—people you may not have known nine weeks ago! We're so proud of you.

You've helped change family trees! Think about that single mom in your class. When you helped her learn how to budget for the first time, you changed her life and the lives of her kids. Think about the young married couple you watched grow together. Because of your influence, they will never have to worry about money fights! Or what about the couple nearing the end of their careers? Your encouragement gave them hope that they'll be able to retire with dignity.

Thank you for joining us in this movement to change lives across the nation . . . one class at a time.

WE ARE ON A MISSION

Did you know there are other ways you can share the life-changing principles learned in *Financial Peace University* with your community? Here are just a few!

Share *Financial Peace for Teens* With Your Youth Ministry

Can you imagine learning the principles of financial peace as a teenager? *Financial Peace for Teens* is specifically designed for youth groups and other youth ministries so teens can learn how to handle money God's ways! Work with your youth leaders to give the kids in your church the gift of starting their adult lives debt-free!

FINANCIAL Peace® FOR TEENS

For more information, visit
coordinatorcentral.com

Bring *Financial Peace University* to Your Entire Church

What if everyone in your church could have financial peace? *Financial Peace ChurchWide* is the tailored plan to take your entire church through *Financial Peace University* at the same time. Imagine the impact a congregation of debt-free, generous givers could have! We encourage you to speak with your pastor to help bring this life-changing movement to your church.

FINANCIAL PEACE ChurchWide

For more information, visit
daveramsey.com/churchwide

Become a Ramsey Solutions Master Financial Coach

How would you like to help people win with money as a financial coach? With our world-class online program, Financial Coach Master Training, you'll learn how to walk someone step by step through their specific financial situation. Whether they're on the verge of bankruptcy or ready for investing, you'll have everything you need to confidently help them solve their financial problems and progress through the Baby Steps! As a coordinator, you've already seen how rewarding it is to help people win with money. Take the next step and become a Ramsey Solutions Master Financial Coach.

FINANCIAL COACH
MASTER TRAINING

For more information, visit
fcmtonline.com

Share SmartDollar With Local Businesses

Did you know that companies can offer Dave's program to their employees as part of their benefits package? SmartDollar is designed specifically for the workplace and is completely online! Based on the same 7 Baby Steps you know and love, it's the best financial wellness solution in the market! Reach even more people in your community by sharing SmartDollar where they work.

smartdollar®

For more information, visit
smartdollar.com

Help Students Learn How to Win With Money

You can help high school and middle school students learn the things about money you wish you knew years ago! Our *Foundations in Personal Finance* curriculum has been taught in more than 40% of high schools across the country and has impacted the lives of more than four million students. Share this curriculum with schools in your community to help students learn how to win with money.

FOUNDATIONS®
in PERSONAL FINANCE

For more information, visit
ramseyeducation.com

LEARN MORE FROM *Dave, Chris, and Rachel!*

Stay connected with our team!

Interested in hearing from us live? Reserve your seat for one of our upcoming live events at **daveramsey.com/events**. If you can't make it in person, host a class and watch one of the livestreams together! (Call your Advisor for details.)

You can also hear from Dave, Chris, and Rachel on their shows:

THE DAVE RAMSEY SHOW

Hear from Dave every weekday on ***The Dave Ramsey Show***—listen on the radio or on our app! (daveramsey.com/show)

THE CHRIS HOGAN SHOW

Learn more from Chris on ***The Chris Hogan Show*** podcast. (chrishogan360.com)

THE Rachel Cruze SHOW™

Watch Rachel on ***The Rachel Cruze Show*** or listen on her podcast. (rachelcruze.com)

SCHEDULE YOUR NEXT CLASS!

We can't host *Financial Peace University* classes without coordinators just like you.

At any given time, classes are offered in over 15,000 churches across the country. And we're always looking for *more* classes to reach even *more* people. That means finding volunteers to become coordinators and asking coordinators like you to lead again!

We know life gets busy, but people in your community are looking for help in their finances—and YOU can help them. We've made it easy for you to schedule your next class from your Coordinator Dashboard! (Or reach out to your Advisor.)

YOU PICK THE TIME

Now that you know what to expect, pick the time of day that works best for your schedule.

YOU PICK THE DATE

Classes can meet year-round. Look at your schedule and set a date that's convenient for you.

YOU PICK THE PLACE

Remember, your next class can meet at a church, a local community center, or even at your home.

Change MORE LIVES!

Go to your Coordinator Dashboard and select "Start a Class" to schedule your next class. Have questions? Don't hesitate to call your Advisor!

BUDGET FORMS & KEY TERMS

(more fun stuff!)

BUDGETING FORMS

Building new budgeting habits is a lot easier with the right tools. That's why we created **EveryDollar**—so you can easily make a plan for your money every month.

If you need a little extra guidance for budgeting weekly or budgeting for irregular income, the following two forms will help you out! Read through the step-by-step instructions on these example forms, then go to **financialpeace.com** to print out blank versions of these forms to fill out yourself.

Hey, Nerds!

If you love pen-and-paper planning, you can find more forms—including extra budgeting forms—at **financialpeace.com**.

DIRECTIONS FOR
ALLOCATED SPENDING *Planning*

If you want to budget based on your pay period rather than the month, this form is for you! The four columns on this form represent the four weeks in a given month. If you're married, combine both of your incomes and then follow the steps below to allocate your spending.

1 FILL OUT YOUR PAY PERIOD DATES AND PAY PERIOD INCOME.

Your **pay period dates** are simply how long you'll go between paychecks. For example, if you get paid on the 1st and 15th, then your pay period for July would be 7/1 to 7/14. Your **pay period income** is how much you will be paid in that pay period. In our example, that will be $3,188.

Pay Period Dates	7/1 TO 7/14
Pay Period Income	$3,188

2 FILL OUT YOUR PLANNED AND REMAINING COLUMNS.

For this pay period, write down how much money **you plan to spend** in each category in the **Planned** column. In the **Remaining** column, keep a running total of how much of your income **you have left** for that pay period.

HOUSING	Planned	Remaining
Mortgage/Rent	$945	$2,243
Water	$25	$2,218

3 PLAN FOR EACH CATEGORY ON THE LIST UNTIL YOU HIT ZERO.

Plan for each category on the list until the Remaining column hits **zero**. When that happens, you're done budgeting for that pay period!

	Planned	Remaining
Saving	$100	$90
Giving	$90	$0

4 IF YOU HAVE MONEY LEFT OVER . . .

If you've planned for every category and you still have money left over in the Remaining column, **go back and adjust an area**, such as savings or giving, so that you spend every single dollar. **Every dollar needs a job to do!**

If the remaining column still has money, adjust an area!

	Planned	Remaining
Saving +$50	$100	$200
Giving +$60	$90	$110

ALLOCATED SPENDING FORM

Don't let this form scare you. Managing your money week to week happens here!

We've made an example form throughout the next couple of pages to help! **For a blank form, go to financialpeace.com.**

Pay Period Dates	7/1 TO 7/14	7/15 TO 7/29	TO	TO
Pay Period Income	$3,188	$472		

Income – Church = Remaining to budget this pay period

GIVING

	Planned	Remaining	Planned	Remaining	Planned	Remaining	Planned	Remaining
Church	$410	$2,778						
Charity								

Remaining minus planned, and then go back & forth

SAVINGS

	Planned	Remaining	Planned	Remaining	Planned	Remaining	Planned	Remaining
Emergency Fund								

HOUSING

	Planned	Remaining	Planned	Remaining	Planned	Remaining	Planned	Remaining
Mortgage/Rent	$945	$1,833						
Water			$55	$417				
Natural Gas			$75	$342				
Electricity	$100	$1,733						
Cable/Internet	$40	$1,693						
Trash								

Pay Period Dates	7/1 TO 7/14		7/15 TO 7/29		TO		TO	

TRANSPORTATION

	Planned	Remaining	Planned	Remaining	Planned	Remaining	Planned	Remaining
Gas	$200	$1,493						
Maintenance								

FOOD

	Planned	Remaining	Planned	Remaining	Planned	Remaining	Planned	Remaining
Groceries	$450	$1,043	$150	$192				
Restaurants	$50	$993						

PERSONAL

	Planned	Remaining	Planned	Remaining	Planned	Remaining	Planned	Remaining
Clothing	$150	$843						
Phone			$124	$68				
Fun Money	$30	$813	$30	$38				
Hair/Cosmetics	$60	$753						
Subscriptions								

LIFESTYLE

	Planned	Remaining	Planned	Remaining	Planned	Remaining	Planned	Remaining
Pet Care								
Child Care								
Entertainment	$50	$703						
Miscellaneous								

Pay Period Dates	7/1 TO 7/14		7/15 TO 7/29		TO		TO	

HEALTH

	Planned	Remaining	Planned	Remaining	Planned	Remaining	Planned	Remaining
Gym								
Medicine/Vitamins								
Doctor Visits	$50	$653						

INSURANCE

When Remaining equals zero, you're done budgeting for this pay period!

	Planned	Remaining	Planned	Remaining	Planned	Remaining	Planned	Remaining
Health Insurance			$38	$0				
Life Insurance								
Auto Insurance	$88	$565						
Homeowner/Renter	$12	$553						
Identity Theft								

DEBT

	Planned	Remaining	Planned	Remaining	Planned	Remaining	Planned	Remaining
Car Payment	$310	$243						
Credit Card 1	$150	$93						
Credit Card 2	$45	$48						
Credit Card 3								
Student Loan								
Medical Bill	$48	$0						
Personal Loan								

DIRECTIONS FOR

IRREGULAR INCOME *Planning*

If your income is different every month, use the Irregular Income Form—along with your EveryDollar budget—to make a plan for your money before the month begins. Follow the steps below to make a plan for any additional income you earn this month.

1 FILL OUT YOUR BUDGET.

Fill out your budget based on **what you reasonably expect to bring home** for the month. If you aren't sure, use last year's lowest income month as your starting point.

INCOME	
Paycheck	$3,500

2 FILL OUT THE ITEMS COLUMN.

In the Items column, list out anything that didn't make it into your budget. These are **items you couldn't budget for,** but you still need to fund.

ITEMS
Main Card - Snowball
Hospital Bill - Snowball
Store Card - Snowball

3 LIST ITEMS IN PRIORITY ORDER.

Make sure your Items list is in the right order and keep a running total. Setting the right **priorities** is crucial here. For instance, a beach trip is not more important than paying off your debt!

PLANNED
$50
$460
$770

4 FILL IN ADDITIONAL INCOME.

When you get paid, write any **additional income** in the box. "Additional" means anything above and beyond what you planned on your budget.

ADDITIONAL IRREGULAR INCOME	$1,500

5 SPEND UNTIL IT'S GONE.

Spend your money right down the list **until it's all gone.** You most likely won't make it all the way down the list. That's okay! That's why it's important to prioritize.

PLANNED	RUNNING TOTAL
$460	+ $510
$770	= $1,280
~~$500~~ $220	~~$1,780~~ $1,500

IRREGULAR INCOME FORM

This form helps you prioritize and plan for the items that didn't make it into your monthly budget. Follow the steps on the previous page to plan for your additional irregular income. We've made an example form below to help! **For a blank form, go to financialpeace.com.**

Any additional irregular income goes here.

ADDITIONAL IRREGULAR INCOME	$1,500

List in priority order anything that didn't make it into your monthly budget.

Work back & forth, adding each budgeted item to the running total.

ITEMS	PLANNED	RUNNING TOTAL
Main Card - Snowball	$50	+ $50
Hospital Bill - Snowball	$460	= $510
Store Card - Snowball	$770	$1,280
Car Sinking Fund	~~$500~~ $220	~~$1,780~~ $1,500
Christmas Sinking Fund	$100	

KEY TERMS

Money shouldn't be complicated. **We make it simple.** We cover the words and phrases used in the last nine lessons in a way that's easy to understand.

SAVING & BUDGETING

Baby Steps: Dave Ramsey's proven seven-step path for winning with money.

Budget: A monthly plan, either on paper or digital, that puts every dollar you make into a specific category.

Compound Interest: Interest that gets paid on both the money you put in (your principal) and on the interest you've already earned.

Four Walls: The most basic expenses you need to cover to keep your family going: your food, your utilities, your shelter, and your transportation.

Interest Rate: An extra percentage you pay to a lender for money you borrow.

Money Market Mutual Fund: Basically, a savings account you can open with a mutual fund company instead of a bank; it usually earns a little more interest than a bank savings account thanks to short-term mutual fund investments.

Sinking Fund: Setting aside money over time so you can buy something with cash—for example, saving $400 a month for 10 months to buy a $4,000 car.

Zero-Based Budget: A monthly budget that puts every dollar you earn into specific categories—so when your income is subtracted from your expenses, you come up with zero.

DEBT

Annual Percentage Rate (APR): The amount that borrowed money costs you each year; the APR includes your interest rate and other related fees you have to pay on a loan.

Debt Snowball: List of all debts (except your house) from smallest to largest. Make minimum payments on all of them while you attack the smallest debt with a vengeance. Once that debt is gone, take that payment and apply it to the second smallest debt. Keep this going until you've paid off the last, largest debt.

FICO Score: Number used to evaluate your "credit worthiness;" it's really an "I love debt" score that's based on your debt history, how much debt you currently have, how long you've been in debt, new debt, and the kind of debt you have.

Introductory Rate: A marketing tool that offers a lower-than-normal interest rate during the early stages of a loan; it's a rate designed to attract new customers, and it almost always goes up over time.

Navient: A student loan service that split off from Sallie Mae in 2013.

Sallie Mae: Originally a government program known as the Student Loan Marketing Association (SLMA), it's still the largest private student loan lender in the country.

SPENDING

Brand Recognition: A marketing term that measures just how aware customers are of particular brands.

Buyer's Remorse: Feeling of doubt or regret about a purchase soon after making it.

Caveat Emptor: Latin term that means "let the buyer beware".

Financing: Using debt to buy something; can also refer to the attractive terms and conditions companies use to market what they want you to buy with debt.

Impulse Purchase: Buying something without thinking about the bigger picture.

INSURANCE

Cash Value Life Insurance: Basically, a permanent life insurance policy (as opposed to a term policy) that charges high premiums and puts money in a savings account with low return rates; also referred to as whole life, universal life, and variable life. Never buy this kind of life insurance.

Claim: The paperwork you send to an insurance company when you want them to cover a loss.

Coverage: The amount of protection you get from an insurance company when you suffer a loss.

Deductible: The money you pay out of pocket before insurance benefits kick in.

Health Savings Account (HSA): A tax-free savings account that sets aside money for medical expenses.

Liability: The amount of your financial obligation when you're found at fault in an accident.

Policy: In insurance, a contract that explains what is covered and what is not.

Premium: The regular payment you make to an insurance company to ensure coverage; can be a monthly, quarterly, or annual payment.

Stop Loss: For insurance, the maximum amount of out-of-pocket expense you pay each year.

Term Life Insurance: Life insurance that remains in force for a certain period (a term); if someone depends on your income, you need term life insurance.

INVESTING

401(k): A retirement savings plan through a business where employees set aside tax-deferred income from each paycheck.

401(k) Match: A company benefit where an employer "matches" a percentage of what an employee sets aside for retirement.

403(b): A tax-favored retirement plan for public school and nonprofit employees.

Roth 401(k): An employer-sponsored retirement plan funded with after-tax money; since taxes have already been paid, the account grows tax-free.

Roth IRA: A personal retirement account that grows tax-free because it's funded with after-tax dollars.

Direct Transfer: Moving the money from one tax-deferred retirement plan into another approved plan; because none of the money goes to you, there are no immediate tax liabilities or penalties. Also known as a "rollover." Often used when moving from one company to another.

Diversification: Spreading money among different kinds of investments to minimize risk.

Individual Retirement Arrangement (IRA): A tax-deferred plan where workers can save some of their income for retirement; as the plan's value grows, the money isn't taxed until it's taken out.

Liquidity: A measure of how easy it is to get to your money from an account; the easier the access, the more liquid it is.

Mutual Fund: An investing tool where a group of people combine their money to create a fund of several different stocks.

Risk: The level of uncertainty about the potential returns on an investment.

Rollover: See "Direct Transfer".

Share: How much an individual investor owns in a publicly traded company.

MORTGAGE

Adjustable-Rate Mortgage (ARM): The mortgage interest rate changes—usually going up—periodically; allows banks to transfer risk to consumers through higher interest rates.

Curb Appeal: How nice a house looks to someone passing by.

Comparative Market Analysis (CMA): The estimated value of property based on what similar properties in the area have sold for.

Equity: How much of property you own compared to how much you still owe on it; usually seen in terms of how much of a mortgage amount you've actually paid.

Fannie Mae (FNMA): The Federal National Mortgage Association, a privately owned company that deals in mortgages.

Fixed Rate: An interest rate that never changes over time; considered a much better option than an adjustable rate.

Inflation Hedge: An asset that increases in value over time and counters a rising inflation rate.

Multiple Listing Service (MLS): A computer program used by real estate agents to search updated property listings.

Mortgage: A loan arrangement made for buying real estate; the property serves as collateral for the loan.

Private Mortgage Insurance (PMI): Insurance that protects a lender from a borrower who defaults on a mortgage; usually required when the borrower has paid less than 20% of the mortgage value.

Principal: For investments, the original amount of money put in the investment; for loans, the actual payoff amount of a loan, not including interest or other fees.

GIVING

Firstfruits: The first produce gathered during a harvest, typically given as an offering to God in the Bible.

Great Misunderstanding: The mistaken belief that you get more by holding tightly to what you have instead of keeping an open hand.

Offering: A gift given above and beyond the tithe; freewill gifts given without a sense of obligation or expectation.

Stewardship: The act of managing the resources God has given each of us for His glory.

Tithe: A gift of the first 10% of one's income, given to the local church.

LEAD LIKE NO ONE ELSE

FPU COORDINATOR

FINANCIAL Peace UNIVERSITY

THERE IS *Ultimately* ONLY ONE WAY TO FINANCIAL PEACE

AND THAT IS TO
Walk Daily
WITH THE
Prince
OF PEACE,
CHRIST JESUS

Budget
Like a
Boss

For more information, please visit our website at daveramsey.com.

$27,275.97 in 7 mnths 5 days!
Andrea and Joshua Hahn
We did this for you Maverick!
Thanks, Dave!

We're DEBT FREE!!
191,300.00 in 10 months
We SOLD our Rental :)
Thank-you Lord!!
Jesse ♡ Carol

We are debt free!
$123,495
Ron & Colleen Barger
THANK YOU DAVE!!!

Nate, Laura, Nathan, Luke, and Rachel McDonell
$96,000 in 37 months!!!
"We're Debt Free!"

$249 K in 4 yrs!
Andrew, Kelly, AJ Weisner
Columbus, Indiana

Jarrod & Stefanie Staggs
122k in 36 months!!
DEBT FREE!!! WOOOO!

FREEDOM!!!
Living like no one else so later we can live like no one else!
22K/18 mos
Cash flowing 20K for school!
Sebastian & Mackenzie Sanchez

Ben & Alyson Baxter
$80,000 in 36 months

Andy From Inwood, WV
$206,000 in 44 months
Love the Financial Peace